# No Regrets

# No Regrets

COLEEN NOLAN

MICHAEL JOSEPH
*an imprint of*
PENGUIN BOOKS

# MICHAEL JOSEPH

Published by the Penguin Group

Penguin Books Ltd, 80 Strand, London WC2R ORL, England

Penguin Group (USA) Inc., 375 Hudson Street, New York, New York 10014, USA

Penguin Group (Canada), 90 Eglinton Avenue East, Suite 700, Toronto, Ontario, Canada M4P 2Y3
(a division of Pearson Penguin Canada Inc.)

Penguin Ireland, 25 St Stephen's Green, Dublin 2, Ireland (a division of Penguin Books Ltd)

Penguin Group (Australia), 707 Collins Street, Melbourne, Victoria 3008, Australia
(a division of Pearson Australia Group Pty Ltd)

Penguin Books India Pvt Ltd, 11 Community Centre, Panchsheel Park, New Delhi – 110 017, India

Penguin Group (NZ), 67 Apollo Drive, Rosedale, Auckland 0632, New Zealand
(a division of Pearson New Zealand Ltd)

Penguin Books (South Africa) (Pty) Ltd, Block D, Rosebank Office Park,
181 Jan Smuts Avenue, Parktown North, Gauteng 2193, South Africa

Penguin Books Ltd, Registered Offices: 80 Strand, London WC2R ORL, England

www.penguin.com

First published 2014

001

Copyright © Coleen Nolan, 2014

The moral right of the author has been asserted

The picture permissions on p. 276 constitute an extension of this copyright page

Set in 14.5/17pt Garamond MT Std
Typeset by Jouve (UK), Milton Keynes
Printed in Great Britain by Clays Ltd, St Ives plc

A CIP catalogue record for this book is available from the British Library

ISBN: 978-0-718-17924-3

www.greenpenguin.co.uk

For my children, Shane, Jake and Ciara. You are and always will be my greatest achievement. I hope when you read this book you'll learn that life throws many obstacles in your path. You will make mistakes along the way – everybody does. But as long as you learn from them, it's OK to move on. Some decisions will be hard to make and some will be easy, and all will lead you to the path you are meant to be on. There will be times when you may wish you had done things differently but I hope that, like me, you will look back one day and say, 'I have no regrets.'

# Foreword

A single spotlight shines down on our family's brightest star. The pencil-slim beam falls on to a stand of radiant lilies and, next to them, the coffin of our beloved sister. It seems madness that I'm sitting here, in Blackpool's Grand Theatre, saying goodbye to Bernie. But here I am.

My hands grip the arms of the seat in the theatre stalls and crush the velvet. The auditorium is dark, making the drama of the spotlit casket on the stage all the greater. Outside it's a sunny July day, one of the hottest of the year, but in the theatre there is a chill. Or perhaps it's just me. My fingers are freezing and my hands are shaking. It's as if my body has slowed its circulation to reflect the sombre mood.

A photograph of Bernie is shining from a screen on the backdrop of the stage. She's looking straight out at us, her blue eyes sparkling with defiant life. Her hair, blonde and shiny, sweeps across her face and she rests her chin on her left hand. This is the Bernie I remember, although other, earlier, black-and-white memories flood back, too.

Bernie aged six, grabbing hold of my two-year-old toddler chubby cheeks. She had an absolute infatuation with my cheeks that drove me insane. She'd pinch them between her thumbs and forefingers and rub her face against mine. When you're a kid you think, Get off, you weirdo! I'd often see her come into a room and I'd leg it because I knew she'd make a beeline for me. 'Ooh, but your cheeks are so soft!' she'd say. To be honest, she was still doing it when we were grown women. If it was weird when I was a kid, it was down-right embarrassing in my forties.

Bernie playing Miss World on our steps in Black-pool, with me, my sister Linda and our next-door neighbour Suzanne. We'd make ballgowns and sashes out of tea towels, and crowns out of cardboard, and take turns to be the announcer, the judge and the win-ner. As the youngest I very rarely won – I was just happy they let me play with them.

Bernie in the bedroom next to mine, singing day and night into a hairbrush and practising her moves in the mirror. Even then she had such an amazing voice. She'd keep me awake pretending to be Lulu and sing-ing, 'We-e-e-e-e-e-e-ll, you know you make me wanna shout!' I'd bang on the wall and tell her to shut up – even though I loved listening to her.

Bernie going through the horrendous loss of her stillborn baby, Kate. She'd carried her for six months, and when she died, Bernie was forced to deliver her knowing the worst had happened. It rocked the whole family. She and her husband Steve were so strong and dignified, keeping their grief quite private.

Bernie getting her big TV acting break as a main character in *Brookside*. I was so excited although filled with nerves. What would I say to her if she was a bit crap? I needn't have worried – as with everything Bernie did, she gave it her all. She was brilliant in *Brookside* and later in *The Bill*.

To my left I can just make out the profile of my sister Anne. She's the oldest of us girls, the one we look to at times like this. It's been a while since we've been so close but right now all the arguments, all the bickering, seem a very long way behind us. She's sitting close to Denise and I can see they're holding hands. Heartbroken together.

To my right sits Linda and, next to her, Maureen. We're as close as sisters can be but at this moment we need our space. If our eyes meet it will be too awful. I steal a glance and see that Maureen's face is wet with tears.

In the front row sit Steve and Erin. Bernie's husband and little girl. Steve has wrapped his arms around his daughter, as if to protect her from the ordeal of having to let her mum go. It kills me to look at them. The pain in Erin's face just breaks my heart. Bernie, Bernie, Bernie. I have so many memories of her. That's why it seems impossible that I'm here right now.

The screen has come alive and Bernie is singing. She's standing on a stage, in front of hundreds of fans, doing her version of Whitney Houston's 'Run To You'. I grip the velvet arms of the seat more tightly but it's no good. The waves of grief are now so huge. What will I do when the music stops and the lights come on?

From alongside me comes the answer. My husband Ray, himself shattered by grief but trying hard to be strong, takes my left hand and slips his other arm around my shoulders. I lean into him, letting him take my weight, burying my face in the dark material of his best suit. His hand goes to my hair and strokes it, soothing me. He presses his lips to my ear and tells me everything will be OK.

Now the lights are on and people around us are standing and making their way outside. It seems a long time since I've even been conscious of my legs and feet but now I must use them. Slowly, and very cautiously, I press the seat arms to push myself up. Big mistake. My legs aren't ready and I can feel myself slumping back into the chair.

'Here, grab hold of my arm,' Ray whispers. He pulls me to my feet and holds me up, letting me hide my mascara-streaked face in his chest.

This is it, I think. This is what's important. Feeling such sorrow because you've felt such love. Feeling like you want to grab every minute you can with your family because life can be too short. And feeling safe in the arms of the man you love and who loves you, for better or for worse.

With baby steps, we move towards the exit . . .

# Chapter One

So, imagine the scene. I'm balancing on two razor-sharp blades on a cruel, hard, icy surface, my tiny diamanté costume revealing more of me than anyone would comfortably wish to see. Five famous faces are about to pass judgement on my performance and seal my fate in front of millions of people. Yes, I was about to be kicked off the 2009 series of *Dancing On Ice*, live on national television . . . and I couldn't have been happier!

'I think I've challenged myself enough now!' I told Ray, on the night I eventually bowed out from ITV's skating show. And, my God, did I mean it! For six months I'd pushed my poor body to its absolute limits and been in a constant state of terror.

The training had been difficult enough. I'd never skated in my life before my patient coach, Donna, had used every trick in the book to coax and cajole me on to the ice at a rink in Manchester. As if that wasn't enough, I was also working on my DVD *Discoburn*. The training for that and *Dancing On Ice* left me almost crying with exhaustion. Oh, and did I mention the other jobs? Full-time mum, *Loose Women* presenter, and weekly magazine and newspaper columnist? It was, as they say, quite a juggle.

By the time we reached the live televised *Dancing*

*On Ice* shows in January 2009, I was in an absolute state. I know plenty of people work hard. There are women who do real jobs, like nursing or teaching or working in a factory. They might find it difficult to believe that my line of work can make you feel as weary as any of those roles. But, honestly, there were times I would be sitting on the Euston to Manchester train just crying my eyes out. I'm not exaggerating when I say I was heading for a nervous breakdown. I really think I was. I'd be running to meet a journalist in a hotel to do an interview, then I'd be training on the ice and after that I'd be rushing to the studios to film *Loose Women*. I'd never worked so hard in my life.

It wasn't as if I could afford to take any shortcuts so far as the ice skating was concerned. I knew that most of the other celebrities were way better than me to begin with, and they were all training more often. Plus, I was still so heart-stoppingly terrified of skating I would feel physically sick every time I put on the boots.

I'd never known fear like it. As soon as I drove into the car park of the ice rink I could feel my heart rate quicken. My palms were wet before I even got out of the car. You know that awful Sunday-night feeling in the pit of your stomach that we used to have as school kids? Well, that was what it was like for me every night before I skated. I think I would have done almost anything rather than step out on to the ice.

Some nights I'd keep poor Ray awake as nightmares caused me to toss and turn and scream in my sleep. In one dream I was standing alone in the middle of a massive ice rink. I knew that somewhere, beyond the blackness of the ringside, there were cameras beaming my picture to an enormous TV audience. The lights go on, the music starts and I do . . . nothing. I'm frozen to the ice in fear, my lovely partner Stuart Widdall nowhere to be seen. Another night I dreamed I was using a trapeze above the ice rink. I'd do a couple of twists and somersaults, and suddenly I was flying through the air, hurtling towards the ice without Stuart's strong arms to catch me. But the very worst nights were those when I simply couldn't fall asleep. I'd lie there in the darkness next to Ray, begging sleep to take me, and wondering why on earth I'd let myself be persuaded to do such an idiotic thing in the first place.

There were so many times that I almost admitted defeat and begged my agent, Neil Howarth, to get me out of it. And there were so many reasons to want to run away. The five a.m. starts, the bruised ribs, the strain on my poor old knees were enough on their own to make me want to give up. But each time I decided enough was enough, that I had to quit, something stopped me.

Perhaps it was the sight of my daughter Ciara, who was eight at the time, and her daddy sitting in the audience each Sunday night. I could hear them cheering my name and waving banners of support, both looking as proud as Punch.

'I'm so pleased you're doing this, Mum,' Ciara would tell me each week, after I'd survived to skate another day. 'I don't think you'll ever get voted off.'

And then there were the times I'd catch Ray fighting back tears, so moved was he by my performances. He knew more than anyone else what it took for me to be out there – he didn't care how good (or bad) I was, he was impressed by what he saw as my bravery.

As somehow I stayed in week after week, Ciara and Ray were joined by other friends and family members. My sons Shane Junior and Jake came to watch their mum face her fears. And three of my sisters, Bernie, Linda and Maureen, were also there each weekend. It felt so amazing, cutting across the ice to the sound of our biggest hit single, 'I'm In The Mood For Dancing'.

'Oh, my God, I can't believe that's you out there!' said Linda, after I'd managed to escape the skate-off yet again.

Sarcasm comes easier than compliments to us sisters. 'It must be easier than it looks!' laughed Bernie. But I was grateful for their support. With Maureen, Linda and Bernie behind me, I was invincible. 'Keep on doing what you're doing!' they urged.

Then there were the lovely folk at home who were kind enough to lift their phones and vote for me. Honestly, at times it felt like the entire country was roaring me on. I just couldn't let everyone down.

By week nine I was beginning to gain some confidence when disaster struck. Stuart and I were rehearsing our routine on the rink at Elstree studios when one of our moves went wrong. My foot slipped from under me and I could see I was about to land badly on the ice. I put out my hand to break my fall and crack! I felt a sickening crunch and I knew that this time I'd really hurt myself. It turned out I'd fractured my thumb and Sharon, the show's physio, wasn't sure if I should carry on. Suddenly, after wanting to run away from the show I was desperate to stay in.

Ciara's going to be so disappointed, I thought. And the truth was, I would be, too.

Our weekend routine saw Ciara and Ray travelling to Elstree on a Friday evening where we'd treat ourselves to a hotel. I loved that. I think they knew that some of my terrors would disappear, the closer I was to them. But this time, when they arrived, Ciara was upset that my hand was wrapped in bandages.

'Are you going to have to give up, Mum?' she asked, trying to look brave.

That was the kick up the bum I needed.

'Absolutely not, love,' I said, pulling her towards me and kissing the top of her head. 'They're going to rebuild me, just you wait and see!'

Thankfully, Sharon was able to strap me up in time for the Sunday. Dressed in a black sequinned outfit and dancing to 'Diamonds Are Forever', I had renewed determination. The judges – Karen Barber, Nicky Slater, Jason Gardiner, Ruthie Henshall and Robin Cousins – awarded us our highest score yet and, to my utter joy, I was through to the last four.

'Oh, my God, oh, my God!' I screamed to Ray, in the bar after the show. 'We're in the semi-final! I just can't believe it!' Maybe I can actually do this! I thought, hardly daring to dream.

So, now there were just four of us left standing. Tough investigative reporter Donal MacIntyre, the graceful and willowy former Liberty X singer Jessica Taylor, eventual winner and all-round box of talent Ray Quinn . . . and me! But my luck was about to run out and, pretty soon, even standing would be unbearable.

If Stuart and I made it to the final we would have to perform a flying routine where I'd be attached by wires to a special harness. This is just like one of those nightmares, I thought. I'd spent the evening with living legends Jayne Torvill and Christopher Dean as they showed me how to fly through the air like a trapeze artist. Oh, my God, I can't believe I'm doing this, I thought. A few weeks ago I didn't even know how to put my skates on – now I was actually turning somersaults! It was such a thrill and truly exhilarating. But, as so often happens, pride came before a fall. I was just beginning to feel a little pleased with myself when there was a sudden and definite twang in my back. I soldiered on, turning another five somersaults, until I felt a gripping spasm shooting along my spine.

'Get me down! Get me down, please,' I cried. The team quickly lowered me but as soon as they removed the harness the agony kicked in. The pain was even worse than childbirth. It was excruciating. The paramedics got me to Barnet Hospital where I was given a full check-up and some strong painkillers. But despite the best efforts of the fantastic physios, my back was in almost permanent spasm. At one point the pain was so bad it actually made me throw up. After so many months spent looking for a way out, no one would have blamed me for retiring hurt. But, just like the week before when I'd fractured my thumb, I knew I didn't want to.

The next day, in a desperate attempt to get me moving again, Sharon gave me five and a half hours of intense physio. The following morning I awoke to more spasms but she soon arrived to give me further treatment and to strap up my back to protect it.

'I'm prepared to let you have a go at training tomorrow,' she said, 'but take it gently – one step at a time.'

Well, I could have kissed her! I spent the rest of the week grimacing with pain as I grabbed every moment on the ice that I could. I'd have to stop each hour for more physio but it was enough for Stuart and me to rehearse a simple routine. I was desperate to make it to the Sunday so that I could skate one last time. It became even more important once I'd hit on the idea of dancing to Shania Twain's 'You're Still The One'. It was the song I'd sung to Ray on our wedding day two years earlier. Strapped up, filled with painkillers and bursting with grim determination to get through the routine, I could hardly wait to be on the ice.

It had meant so much that the people at home had voted for me, week in and week out, that I wanted my time on *Dancing On Ice* to finish on a high.

The day before the semi-final I took a long look in the mirror at my bruised and battered body. It was as if I had war wounds. My arms and legs were yellow, purple and green, testament to the ordeal I had put them through. I knew that the next day would bring with it my very last performance and I was – what? Happy? Yeah, I think I was. I'd faced my demons. I'd spent my forty-fourth birthday being manipulated by a physio. I ached in parts of my body I hadn't felt for years! But I'd proven to myself and to my children that anything is possible and that it's never too late to learn another skill.

On that final night Ray couldn't hold in the tears any longer. As I skated to our wedding song he was in floods. I know this because the cameras kept zooming in on him, much to his embarrassment. We still tease him about the time he blubbed on national TV!

But, lovely as that last routine was, I knew it was time to go and leave it to the other three, who really did know how to skate.

'I'm so out of the competition – we shouldn't even waste time,' I joked to the presenter Phillip Schofield, as he asked the judges for their comments. 'Just bring on the flowers!'

The five judges were kind – even Jason! – and in the days that followed I received so many supportive letters from members of the public that I couldn't have felt more loved.

*Dancing On Ice* showed me that what's important in life is not just being the best but trying your best. I'd practised what I'd preached. And for that I was pretty proud of myself.

If anyone had ever told me that by the spring of 2009 I would have published a number-one best-selling book, be splashed each week on the front cover of millions of women's magazines and be presenting a serious prime-time ITV documentary, I'd have told them they were insane!

And yet, following *Dancing On Ice*, I was about to have the busiest – and most successful – year of my life.

I'd always worked hard. It seems incredible to me now but I started my singing career aged two when I performed on stage with the rest of my family, touring working men's clubs and hotels all over the country. Mum and Dad, my two brothers and five older sisters were known as Blackpool's own von Trapp family, as in *The Sound of Music*. We'd do four turns a week as well as fitting in school. It sounds tough but I never knew any different – I was a Nolan and my future was already mapped out.

Some of my friends had the sort of parents who pushed them at school. But my childhood was very different. Mum and Dad never went to a parents' evening and if I ever dared to dream about following a different path – like becoming a secretary or a teacher – they'd look at me as if I was crazy. My life was already defined and I was going to be a singer – like it or not. I can remember being about five years old and feeling sick with exhaustion after a gig. I would sing something like 'Show Me The Way To Go Home' and sleep in the car afterwards, the streetlights passing overhead. I'd slip into such a deep sleep that it would be torture waking up for school the next day. Sometimes my parents would phone in and make some excuse about me being ill so that I didn't have to go. Is it any wonder I'm not a brain surgeon?

I think back now about my unconventional childhood and I know I'd never allow Ciara to do the same. Luckily she's not showing the slightest interest in following me into the family business so perhaps I don't need to worry. Actually, she's got a lovely voice but I hate the thought of her not having a proper education or being tired like I was. The truth is, things are very different, these days, and Ciara has far more of a say than I ever did.

I was no stranger to grafting but 2009 was something else. I'd never known hard work like it and it felt as if everyone was suddenly very interested in me. In this business you never look a gift horse in the mouth so I found myself saying yes to all the amazing opportunities that were coming my way.

*Loose Women*, which I'd been part of since 2000, was doing really well. Its format of down-to-earth female celebrities chatting with humour and warmth about the topics of the day was a real hit with women (and lots of men!) all over the country. I've always believed it's because the audience loved the panelists and identified with things that were going on in their lives. Women like Kaye Adams, Lynda Bellingham, Sherrie Hewson and Carol McGiffin had become their TV friends, and along the way they were joined by Zoë Tyler, Denise Welch, Jane McDonald, Lesley Garrett and Lisa Maxwell. I was really proud to be part of the *Loose Women* gang.

Much to the delight of all of us girls, the show kept on scooping awards for best daytime programme. We'd love dressing up and attending the likes of the *TV Quick* or National Television Awards to collect our trophies and behave badly! For some reason those awards shows always brought out the naughty side of us and we'd be splashed across the newspapers the next day looking a little the worse for wear. I can't even blame the alcohol as I don't really enjoy getting drunk, but put us together on a night out and we'd somehow manage to get into trouble.

I remember one awards do in 2008 at London's Grosvenor House Hotel. We'd been nominated for Best Daytime Programme but lost to *Come Dine With Me*. By the time they announced the winner we were all slightly trolleyed – even me. After that it was a bit of a blur. Andrea McLean and I were standing in the foyer waiting for our cabs when Carol McGiffin staggered over to us.

'Look at all those photographers,' she said, peering outside. 'I'm going to give them something to photograph.' And with that she rushed outside, pulled up her dress and flashed her lacy black knickers. I could hardly believe what I was seeing. Next Denise Welch got involved and flashed her knickers too – only this time, instead of sexy undies, she revealed flesh-coloured support Spanx! The next thing I knew I had a pencil stuffed into my cleavage and Andrea was being photographed as her boobs fell out of her dress! It was carnage. The following day the *Daily Mail* ran a story: 'LOOSE WOMEN RUN WILD, FLASHING BOTTOMS AND FLESH-COLOURED SUPPORT UNDERWEAR'. It wasn't very dignified.

Despite the misbehaviour, it was lovely going up to collect our awards. But the best part of winning was knowing that the viewers were voting for us. It was good to feel they were rooting for us every step of the way.

Travelling from my home in Wilmslow to spend a few days filming in London every week was tough, though. We'd moved from Blackpool to the Cheshire countryside the year before, after falling in love with the area while visiting Denise Welch and her then husband Tim Healy. It was the best move we ever made and I loved my life there, with our dogs, the horses at the local stables and the friends we'd made in the village.

The house, a double-fronted place with four bedrooms, a cosy sitting room and a huge family kitchen, was surrounded by fields, trees and winding roads, and was a million miles away from anything I had ever known. Every time I went down the gated drive I reminded myself how lucky I was. This is what I'm working for, I told myself.

Nevertheless I hated leaving Ray and Ciara and – when they were home – Shane Junior and Jake, but I was loving my growing career so I worked hard to balance it with family life. Like I said, you've got to grab it when you can.

While I'd been training for *Dancing On Ice* I was also writing my autobiography, *Upfront & Personal.* It told the story of my childhood in Blackpool with my five sisters and two brothers, our singing success with The Nolans and how we'd gone on to tour with Frank Sinatra, appeared on *Top of the Pops* in the eighties and been crazily successful in Japan. The book told of my rocky marriage to *EastEnders'* actor Shane Richie, who'd left me literally holding the babies while he went off on tour and eventually had an affair. It told of the horrible rows I'd had with my eldest sisters Anne and Denise and how I'd met, fallen in love and married a certain musician called Ray Fensome. It included my highlights – definitely the births of my three children – and the low points, such as my constant weight battle, and chronicled the bumpy emotional journeys that had peppered the course of my life.

By April 2009 it was finally published and it felt like such an achievement. It was the first time I'd written anything like it and, to be honest, I was quite proud of myself. One day I was walking past the window of an upmarket bookstore when I saw *Upfront & Personal* centre stage of the shop window. I gave a little squeal of delight and it was all I could do to stop myself rushing in and buying it! To my absolute joy and surprise, *Upfront & Personal* went straight to the top of the best-seller list and stayed there for several weeks. It was wonderful knowing that so many women had found it helpful in their own lives: I had sackful upon sackful of letters, especially from women in their forties.

Many said they had been inspired by the way I had bounced back after the terrible break-up with Shane. It gave me a lovely warm feeling to know that so many people were interested in my life – especially now it definitely appeared to be on the up!

It seemed that finally I had the ideal work-life balance and my profile was higher than it had been in a long while. It was time to look for a bigger television project that I could sink my teeth into.

I'm someone who finds it difficult to be serious for too long. We're all like that in our family: every one of us has the kind of sarcastic sense of humour that makes it difficult ever to have a sensible conversation. My default position is to crack jokes and mess about on screen, so I couldn't blame the television bosses for not giving me anything too serious. But the truth was I'd always secretly wanted to front a prime-time television documentary and I really fancied tackling something heavier and slightly more controversial. Now, suddenly, on the back of my book sales and the success of *Dancing On Ice* and *Loose Women*, I was offered just that. ITV wanted to know if I was interested in making a documentary about the nation's obsession with staying young and staving off the ageing process. I said, 'Let me think about it . . . Erm, YES!'

For years I'd found the trend towards anti-ageing surgery terrifying but at the same time fascinating. I see it a lot in my line of work. I only had to turn my back for two minutes at an awards do to see an old friend with a new face! Here, finally, was the perfect topic for me to begin this new strand of my career, and I couldn't wait to take on the role of hard-hitting investigative reporter. Plus I was curious to see if it was, in fact, possible to grow old gracefully in this day and age.

The programme was to be called *The Truth About Beauty: Eternal Youth* and the producers explained that I would be interviewing other women in the public eye who had chosen to have cosmetic surgery. I'd ask them why they'd decided to take the plunge and how the surgery had made them feel. I'd also chat to doctors and other experts about the latest procedures on offer.

As a woman in her forties living her life in the media spotlight I knew only too well how it felt to be judged by your face, your age and your weight. The emphasis placed on women's appearance is immense and we're constantly criticized – and more rarely praised – for it. Doing my *Discoburn* DVD and taking part in *Dancing On Ice* had recently helped me lose a few stone but that hadn't stopped the odd nasty comment in the newspapers and magazines. Usually the story would run alongside a hilarious photograph of me coming out of the supermarket, my face free of makeup and my hair pulled back in a scrunchie. Then they'd criticize me for not looking my best – thanks a lot!

Sharing the screen with often younger and stunningly beautiful women is enough to shake anyone's confidence and I had, in the past, considered getting a little help from the plastic surgeons. 'Don't be stupid,'

Ray would tell me. 'You're gorgeous exactly as you are.' But then I'd go to work on something like *Dancing On Ice* and stand alongside the goddess who is Holly Willoughby and I'd think, Really? It wasn't a subject to take lightly, though. I needed to know much more about the risks of surgery before making any hasty decisions.

It was the perfect time to do the documentary. *Dancing On Ice* had helped me rediscover my confidence so I thought I was in a good place to take on the challenge. I couldn't have guessed that the experience would unpick almost all that new-found self-assurance and bring back the familiar feelings of self-doubt and insecurity.

Part of the programme involved a computerized age-progression that showed me how I might look in ten and twenty years' time. I'd thought I'd look a bit like my mum, who had beautiful skin, but, my God, it was a terrifying sight. Mum never had a wrinkle, not even in her eighties, but the age progression showed how I would look if I didn't follow in her footsteps. When Auriole had finished she held a mirror up to my face and I had such a shock. It was as if a complete – and very old – stranger was looking back at me.

Still, the shock wasn't enough to make me resort to the surgeon's knife. I'm not against surgery – if that's what you feel you need and you are prepared to take the risks then you should be free to go ahead – but I've always said there's nothing wrong with gaining a few wrinkles on the journey through life. After all, laughter lines are there because you've laughed a lot! Your face tells your life story, good or bad, and the world would be a really boring place if we all looked the same.

God knows I'm not perfect. Like everyone else, I've got my own long list of personal hang-ups and, if it could be done with the wave of a magic wand, I'd be first in the queue for longer legs or perkier boobs. But unfortunately the only fairy godmothers out there wear white doctors' coats – and the wand is scalpel-shaped and part of very expensive and very complex surgical procedures.

The next part of the show would involve me having a consultation with a cosmetic surgeon. He was to examine my face to see what treatment, if any, he would recommend. I should probably have known better, but as I sat waiting for the doctor in his sparkling white clinic, I remember assuming that I didn't really have that much to worry about. I'm not too bad for someone in their mid-forties, I thought. How wrong was I?

The doctor shone a light on to my face. He pulled and prodded my skin, making marks with a felt-tipped pen. 'Well, Coleen,' he started out, kindly enough, 'if you were my client I would be recommending a number of facial procedures. First of all, there are the bags under your eyes. We'd need to do something about them. Then your eyes need to be opened more – I'd suggest a brow lift. Next I'd give you a facial skin peel and finally a basic face lift. Altogether that would cost in the region of twenty thousand pounds.'

What?

'Hang on, hang on!' I said. 'You're only on my face. How much is it going to cost me from the neck down?'

As usual, I made a joke of it but, to be honest, I was utterly devastated. Here was a well-respected doctor pointing out all these things that I had never noticed. Suddenly they were glaringly obvious to me and, to this day, when I look in the mirror, they are the only things I see.

I knew I couldn't go to pieces and that I'd have to finish the documentary but the damage was done. From then on I was constantly asking the makeup girls to check for blemishes and to hide the dark circles under my eyes. The doctor's words would replay over and over inside my head and I couldn't help comparing myself with much younger presenters. But I had to go on. While the cameras were rolling I managed to stay confident and smile my way through to the end of the programme. Inside I was reduced to the insecure person I'd been before I'd lost the weight or worn a spangly costume while dancing on ice.

For a while I considered taking the doctor up on his offer. While filming I'd spoken to so many women who had sworn by their cosmetic surgery and were happy with their new faces. Perhaps he's right. Perhaps I do need £20,000 worth of surgery if I want to stay in this industry, I thought, looking in the mirror and seeing those baggy eyes under droopy brows staring straight back at me.

In the end, a combination of wanting to be around for my kids and absolute cowardice made me realize that plastic surgery was definitely not for me.

At the time the papers were full of the story of poor Denise Hendry, the wife of former Scottish football captain Colin Hendry, who was desperately ill after never fully recovering from botched cosmetic surgery seven years earlier. Denise, aged forty-two, had suffered massive complications and almost died after a liposuction procedure had gone terribly wrong. Months later, in September of that year, she would eventually pass away with a serious infection after undergoing an operation to correct the original surgery. Tragically, she left behind four children aged between nineteen and nine. There isn't a flat tummy in the world that's worth that.

Filming *The Truth About Beauty: Eternal Youth* was an eye opener – in more ways than one. It made me realize how much the cosmetic surgery industry feeds on women's insecurities. When did we all start believing we had to be perfect and hold back the signs of ageing at any cost? I had walked into that doctor's surgery a confident woman and left feeling like the back end of a double-decker bus. Isn't that ridiculous? It's no wonder it's a multi-billion-pound industry – and it goes without saying that, during the course of the programme, I never met a poor consultant!

Not long after the ITV documentary, I had another

major knock to my confidence. And this time it was enough to make me rethink the direction my career was heading in.

Since the success of *Dancing On Ice*, my agent Neil had been getting lots of calls from TV executives expressing their interest. It seemed amazing to me. When life became quieter after the Nolans, I'd been getting on with being there for Ray and the kids. I never dreamed I'd get a second chance at fame. But along came *Loose Women* and suddenly I was in the public eye – albeit a little older and wiser. I'd turned forty before I found myself once again a household name. I had my first magazine cover, on the front of *best*, when I was forty-one, and since then I hadn't looked back. Now I was filming Iceland ads with former Atomic Kitten and *I'm A Celebrity* . . . jungle queen Kerry Katona and doing glamorous swimwear fashion shoots. It really did seem to be my time.

Reaching the semi-finals of *Dancing On Ice* had brought me to the attention of the powers that be. Anyone who saw me in the first few weeks – well, throughout the series, really! – will know that I was most certainly not the fourth-best skater. Much better people, like Melinda Messenger and Zöe Salmon, left the show before I did and that was down to the lovely people at home picking up the telephone and casting their votes for me, week in, week out. When there is a surge of goodwill like that towards somebody, the telly people think, We're on to something here, she's popular, and the telephone in Neil's office had not stopped ringing since.

Who knows why people were voting? Perhaps they were waiting for me to fall over and make a complete fool of myself. But I didn't mind: their support felt like a warm glove and I loved being on prime-time Sunday-night telly.

I was told I was in the running to host another prime-time television programme on a rival network. For the moment it was strictly under wraps but I could tell by the amount of excitement that it was quite a big deal. The executive in charge called me in to have an early chat to see if I would be interested. Despite my continued hang-ups about crow's feet, baggy eyes and droopy brows, I was feeling relatively happy about the success of my first documentary, so I went along with high hopes.

The meeting started well enough. As ever, I was nervous but the executive was very reassuring and said lots of nice things about my TV career so far. He told me a few details about the project and I could feel myself beginning to get swept along by the thought of another prime-time television job. I've been so lucky in my career despite the fact that I'm not ambitious. I'm a great believer in allowing Fate to decide the future – never mind a five-year plan, I don't even have a five-minute plan! So, to be honest, I wasn't knocking on any doors in a desperate bid to get that job. However, if the top brass in TV Land thought I was destined for greater things, who was I to argue?

Suddenly the executive stopped telling me how fantastic I was and said, 'What are you going to do about that?' And, to my horror, he pointed to my tummy.

I laughed nervously and he went, 'No, really, I'm serious. We really like you and we think you'll be great but we have a particular look in mind for the host. Everybody's going on about these gastric bands at the moment, why don't you think about that? Maybe you could do a Fern?'

I've heard about those moments when you feel you're outside your body, looking down on a scene, and that was exactly what happened then. It was as if I was floating in the air above, watching myself and that horrible man below. I couldn't believe what I was hearing.

Twelve months earlier *This Morning* presenter Fern Britton had been at the centre of a row when she had admitted that she'd had a gastric band fitted and that her five-stone weight loss was not due solely to sensible eating and exercise. There was a bit of a stink because some felt Fern, the face of the diet cracker Ryvita, had cheated. Although it has to be said that not everybody disapproved. Fern looked amazing and, despite the outcry, there had been a massive surge of interest in gastric surgery, with some clinics reporting a 400 per cent rise in enquiries. She'd recently announced that she was leaving *This Morning* – and I was being told by a TV boss to 'do a Fern'.

I sat there, open-mouthed, and all the old feelings of insecurity came flooding back. I was so shocked and hurt that I didn't know what to say. To be honest, I was so embarrassed that I wanted to jump out of my seat and run out of the door but fortunately I managed to pull myself together.

I hit back. 'What are you going to do about your face?' I said. 'I've just done a documentary about plastic surgery and I know a good surgeon I could book you in with.'

The man looked at me as if I'd smacked him across the face with a wet fish. His mouth fell open and I saw the tips of his ears turn pink.

'Don't worry, I can see myself out,' I said. Then I stood up and, with as much dignity as I could muster, walked out of the office.

How dare he? It was such a ridiculous thing for him to suggest. Can you imagine an employer in any other industry getting away with that? I'm sure it must be illegal. I was disgusted and angry but, in a way, it was a good thing to have happened. The shock had made it easier for me to walk away and have the confidence to say no to that sort of rubbish.

I'd thought that in this day and age we were over all that. I'd thought we were celebrating women of all ages, shapes and sizes. But not, it seemed, in television where it was still a massive problem. We all know that unless a woman has a certain look she won't be employed for one of the top jobs in television. Look at any TV show and you'll see older men sitting alongside young, slim, beautiful women. Take *Strictly Come Dancing*. Now, I love Len Goodman – in fact, I'm strangely attracted to him but that's another story! There he sits, approaching seventy, alongside the gorgeous Darcey Bussell, and nobody suggests he might need a nip here or a tuck there. Then at *The X Factor* down the years you've had Simon Cowell and Louis Walsh – both brilliant, but neither young nor glamorous. And yet there always also has to be a Cheryl Cole or a Nicole Scherzinger. Admittedly Sharon Osbourne came back in 2013 and she's a real woman – or, at least, several bits of real women!

Still, even if all this was true, there was no way I was going to agree to a gastric band. Don't get me wrong, it's not that I'm violently opposed, they're just not for me. If you're morbidly obese and you've run out of every option then who am I to say, 'Don't do it'? Gastric bands have saved lives, and for lots of people the surgery is their last chance. But you should only do it if you really need to. Sitting there in the TV executive's office, fresh from exposing myself to the nation in no more than a corset, a feather boa and a pair of skating boots, I really didn't think that applied to me.

It's no secret that for twenty-five years I've struggled with my weight. I've written about it in my books and spoken about it on *Loose Women*. I've been up and down those scales like a fiddler's elbow, which is tough when you spend so much time in the public eye.

I started putting on weight after I was married to Shane Richie and gave up my career to look after the boys. I was in an unhappy marriage, Shane was working away all the time and I was at home taking care of toddlers. While he was being mobbed by adoring girl fans, I was feeling fat and frumpy. It sapped my confidence, and the worse I felt the more I comfort-ate. I'd make sure the boys' meals were done but I wouldn't think about what I was going to have. I'd finish off their leftovers or have a bag of crisps. Once they were in bed I'd reach for the biscuit tin and eat until the chocolate Hobnobs made me feel better. I could go for days without seeing anyone other than the children – there didn't seem very much point in making an effort with my weight or appearance. I'd slob around the house in tracksuit bottoms feeling unloved and miserable.

Even when Shane was around I felt invisible. I was so unhappy and my self-esteem at such a low that I couldn't really blame him for not taking any notice of me. I'd think, It's no wonder he doesn't look at me any more. I look crap, I feel crap and I'm knackered. Why on earth would he fancy me?

Once upon a time Shane would have pulled me on to the sofa for a cuddle and to watch a film. But he seemed repulsed by me. It was as if he couldn't stand to be next to me for even a few minutes.

'You don't fancy me any more, do you Shane?' I'd ask him. Unfortunately his answers were never convincing. Fed up with my widening thighs and chubby face, I'd tell him, 'I feel fat.'

He'd just answer, 'Well, why don't you try losing some weight?' For someone who was already feeling vulnerable, it was heartbreaking. I can't tell you what it did for me, a few years later, to read an interview with Shane in which he admitted he'd been a complete git.

'Coleen had done nothing wrong,' he said. 'For a while I used to tell her she'd put on weight, that she didn't understand me. But it was the usual rubbish. It wasn't true. It's just the knee-jerk defence of blokes who have affairs.'

At my heaviest – and unhappiest – I was a size twenty. I really didn't get to grips with my weight until I met Ray, rediscovered my confidence and started mending my career. There's no incentive to lose weight quite like having to watch yourself on screen. Television puts about ten pounds on you and appearing on *Loose Women* motivated me to do something about my weight problem. The scriptwriters on *Coronation Street* seemed to be keeping tabs on me. One day, Vera Duckworth had said something like, 'Is *Loose Women* on today? I like that chubby Nolan.' I laughed at the time but it was another blow to my confidence.

The first thing I did to sort my life out was to go with Ray on a 400-kilometre five-day bike ride along the river Nile to raise money for the Alzheimer's Society. It seemed fitting to raise money to help find a cure for the disease that had blighted Mum's life. There was many a day when my thighs chafed and my legs were too wobbly to pedal, but somehow we managed. It was an amazing moment to cross the finish line alongside my husband – and it was the start of my weight-loss journey.

Next I followed the Rosemary Conley programme. The pressure was on because after I'd tried the diet for a few months I was booked to record my fitness DVD. I started with aerobic workouts three times a week at home, then began to add in sit-ups to tone my tummy and use water bottles as weights. By the time I reached the size-twelve goal for my wedding day, I had lost around five stone. At my lightest I was a size ten.

OK, so my weight had levelled off since then, but at the time the TV executive suggested I have a band fitted, I was a size fourteen, nowhere near a candidate for gastric surgery. It would have been completely unhealthy for someone of my weight and shape to take such drastic action.

I thought again about Denise Hendry and was more convinced than ever that there was no way I'd risk an unnecessary procedure for the sake of my looks and career. I knew, with absolute certainty, that my first responsibility was to Ray, Ciara, Shane Junior and Jake. I wasn't going to put my life on the line for anyone – least of all an unreconstructed little man with a bad attitude towards women!

I was worried, too, for Ciara. As a mum, you walk a fine line between keeping your children fit and healthy and not allowing them to obsess about their weight. I've heard about so many girls of Ciara's age with body issues, eating disorders and low self-esteem. It doesn't help that they spend much of their time taking pictures of themselves to put on the internet – it's like a mania with them. Whenever Ciara mentions body weight I always say, 'It's not about weight, it's about health.' So, yes, I'm happy for her to cut out the chocolate and the pizza but the last thing I want is for her to be conscious of her body shape. She's only twelve: she shouldn't even be thinking about it.

Suddenly I was questioning my new-found determination to take on prime-time television. Was it right for me? Was I right for it? And, if I did get pushed further into the limelight, was I prepared for the pressures of greater fame and constant press criticism about my appearance? You can never get it right with the press. You're either too fat or too thin or too old or too knackered-looking. Knocked about by headlines such as 'COLEEN'S DIET BATTLES' and – at the other end of the scale – 'COLEEN'S DIET TOO FAR', would I end up obsessing about my body, too? What sort of example would that set for Ciara?

When I finally admitted to myself that prime time wasn't what I wanted, it was as if a ton of bricks was taken from my shoulders. I was desperate to spend more time with Ray and the kids. I stopped looking for new television projects and started focusing more on being a mum. Luckily, I still had *Loose Women* to keep me busy for two days a week. Daytime television had always been my natural habitat and now it felt like a safe and family-friendly place to be.

Plus something else was brewing that made the decision to walk away a little easier. For several months now Neil had been talking about the possibility of a reunion tour with my sisters. We hadn't sung or toured together for years and the prospect was really exciting. 'How do you like the sound of that?' he'd asked. Well, I loved the sound of it and, what was more, so did the rest of the girls!

We'd been asked to reunite for tours on many occasions in the past, but for one reason or another it had never been the right time. The girls were usually touring with musicals and stage shows and I had my TV stuff. But suddenly there was a window and a reason for doing it. Unbelievably, it had been thirty years since the success of 'I'm In The Mood For Dancing' and it seemed the perfect time for the Nolans to take to the stage again.

'I'm not getting too excited until I know it's happening,' I said to Linda. The thought of spending a few weeks on the road with my sisters was really appealing and I didn't want to be disappointed.

Then, one day, my phone buzzed and I looked to see who the text was from. It was Neil. *I hope your singing voice is in good shape*, he said, *because I've got amazing news. The tour is on!*

# Chapter Two

It's hard to put into words how we felt that October night in Nottingham on the first night of our I'm In The Mood Again tour. Excited, ecstatic, extremely frightened: we were all of those things. But most of all Linda, Bernie, Maureen and I felt alive, and we couldn't wait to get on stage.

The tour was a chance for us to celebrate the thirtieth birthday of the Nolans' biggest and best-loved hit, 'I'm In The Mood For Dancing'. It's a funny thing about that song. It has haunted all of us throughout our lives, ever since it was released in December 1979. It received loads of attention and radio play, peaking at number three and staying in the charts for fifteen weeks. The charts are very different nowadays and records don't sell nearly as many copies as they used to. But back then 'I'm In The Mood' was an absolute blessing for us. In Japan it reached number one, which was unusual for an English-language song, and it launched a run of amazing success for us over there. At one stage, when I was still a teenager, we were mobbed there. It was crazy. We couldn't leave the hotel and needed the army to escort us everywhere. We even sang the song on television in Japanese! Sometimes I think I'd be happy never to hear it again in my life but, really, I love it. You can't knock what's made you famous. With Bernie's soaring lead vocals, 'I'm In The Mood' had always been so special for us and its anniversary seemed the perfect excuse for one almighty party.

The last and final formation of the Nolans – Linda, Maureen, Bernie and I – hadn't performed together for more than a quarter of a century. My own career had taken a different route entirely, focusing more on TV presenting, and I hadn't sung live for about seventeen years. Life had moved on and we knew that this tour was going to be very different from what we were used to.

In the early days of the Nolans we were expected to do everything ourselves. There were no hairdressers or costume designers running around to make our lives easier. We'd organize our clothes, do our own hair and makeup, choreograph our dance routines and try not to get tangled up in our long microphone wires. When I think back to some of the horrendous outfits we ended up in! Now, the record company Universal was proposing a £2 million all-singing all-dancing production at huge arenas, complete with amazing stage sets, wireless radio mics, top stylists and makeup artists. We could hardly believe what we were hearing.

From the start, though, we had a horrible dilemma. Universal was adamant that it wanted only four sisters on stage. They had done their research and looked up who had been in the line-up during the band's most successful period. 'I'm In The Mood' had really sealed our success and the record company wanted the same formation to do the tour. Although Anne had recorded the song she'd left straight after to have her daughter. During the two years she was away Linda, Maureen, Bernie and I had had hits all over the world, sold more than 25 million records and had been bigger than the Beatles in Japan. She hadn't been involved in our later hits, like 'Gotta Pull Myself Together' and 'Who's Gonna Rock You?' and the record company decided they just wanted the four of us. We all immediately asked them to reconsider and let us do it as a five-piece, but at the end of the day every girl means more costs. We each had our own hairdressers, makeup artists, hotel costs, etc. so they were certain they didn't want to extend the line-up. We knew we had to accept it or let the biggest opportunity the Nolans had had in a long time pass us by.

'Bloody hell, Col, that's really awful for Anne,' Linda said to me, when we first heard the news. 'But, you never know, maybe she'll be OK with it. She might understand.' But Anne didn't understand and she made her feelings very clear.

I know Bernie and Maureen were especially upset for Anne. Bernie tried to reason with Universal and begged the bosses there to reverse their decision. She hated arguing with her sisters and the bad vibes were upsetting for her.

'Look,' she said to Anne, 'if I were a millionaire I'd tell them where to shove it, but I'm just like the rest of us. I need the money.'

'Your loyalties should be with the family, not the record company,' Anne said to her. But there was nothing Bernie could do. No matter how we argued, it was the four of us Universal wanted and the bosses there weren't going to be persuaded otherwise. It was either take it or leave it and we knew we didn't have a choice – but it was a decision that caused the family to split into two camps for many years to come.

Relations were already a bit frosty between myself, Anne and Denise. Back in 2006, when I was commuting up and down to London to do *Loose Women*, I was finding it difficult to employ a nanny to look after Ciara when Ray was busy with work. One day I called Anne to ask her if she had any ideas and she suddenly put herself up for the job. 'Would you think about letting me look after Ciara?' she asked. 'To be honest, I could do with the cash.'

I knew that money was tight for her and that she was going through a difficult divorce with her husband, Brian, but I hadn't considered asking her before because I didn't want to offend her. Would she really want to work for her little sister? By the time I was born Anne was fifteen and it was like having a second mum. As I grew up she would spend hours playing with me and braiding my hair into perfect plaits. The thought now that I would be paying her to look after my own child was really quite odd.

When Anne later rocked the family with her revelations that she had been abused by our dad, Tommy, it was me who supported her. I'm a firm believer that family secrets should not be brushed under the carpet and I thought it would help her cope with what had gone on. In fact, I even helped her find a publisher for her book, *Anne's Song*. By then, we'd lost both Mum and Dad but it was still an awful thing to have gone through. Other members of the family and all of our fans were shocked and saddened. But although I still love my dad to this day, I believe Anne did the right thing in writing that book. We had always shared a close bond and, when I needed her to help me with Ciara, I was touched and pleased that she wanted to be involved.

'Yeah, of course,' I told her, after I'd spoken to Ray. 'I'd love it. I couldn't think of anyone I'd rather leave Ciara with.'

So that was what happened. Anne came over to help out, looking after Ciara when Ray was away and taking care of the house when he was working from home. Ciara loved having her auntie Anne around and at first it seemed like the perfect arrangement. But Anne and Ray would often clash over the silliest things and I'd come home to find there had been a bust-up. Anne was always the feisty one, the leader of the girls' gang when we were kids. And Ray isn't backward in coming forward when he needs to speak his mind. They'd often squabble and I'd be met at the front door by one of them grumbling about what the other had done or said.

'He's driving me mad,' Anne would say. 'I don't know how you put up with him.' I'd humour her because I knew that secretly they were very fond of one another. I'd just knock their heads together and tell them to get over it.

Then one day a trivial row led to an almighty stalemate and began what was to become almost eight years of ill feeling. Ray had been helping Anne's daughters, Amy and Alex, because they were interested in getting into showbusiness. He'd been so encouraging, helping them find auditions and putting them in touch with useful people. Well, showbusiness is tough to get into and things didn't quite work out for them. Eventually the girls decided to give up their ambitions and settle for nine-to-five jobs. When Anne told Ray he couldn't hide his disappointment from her.

'I reckon they're really talented,' he said. 'But in the end they just can't be arsed, can they?'

As soon as he said it there was uproar. Anne was furious and accused Ray of interfering and pushing the girls into something they didn't want to do. She said he had bullied Amy and Alex, and was shouting and screaming at him like she was mad. Then Ray did a stupid thing. He laughed at her and scuttled out of the room to hide in his office. A few moments later Anne followed him in, determined to continue the row. She told him that he and I, Linda and her late husband (who, confusingly, like my brother and Anne's ex, was called Brian) were all backstabbers. It was as if she had been burning with resentment for years, yet for us it came like a bolt from the blue. We'd only ever tried to support her, particularly through her divorce, and to this day none of us can understand where her anger came from. She was digging up all kinds of accusations, pointing the finger at us for this and that. In the end Ray told her that she needed to go home.

I was still in London working when she called me later to tell me she and Ray had fallen out. 'He doesn't want me to come back but I don't want to leave you in the lurch,' she said, sounding upset. 'I just wanted to let you know that I can still have Ciara round at mine if you want.'

'OK,' I said, thinking it didn't sound too serious. In any case, I'd heard it all before. 'I'm sure it'll blow over. I'll give you a call tomorrow.'

As I put the key in the front door Ray met me in the hallway. 'Anne and me had a big row today,' he said, looking a bit sheepish.

'I know,' I said. 'What are you two like?'

The following night Ray and I went to the *Loose Women* wrap party in London. It's a do they always put on to mark the end of the series and we had a great time. We were on the train home when I received a text from my sister Denise, inviting me to her house for a girlie night in with some of the family – Anne, our auntie Theresa and Alex. I was feeling knackered, so I thanked her, made my excuses and told her to have a brilliant night. I was also a bit worried about the row between Anne and Ray. It was relatively fresh and probably best left alone for a while. *Perhaps it's better if I don't come because of the situation*, I wrote. *Let's just let things settle down and I'll be in touch.*

The next thing I knew my phone was buzzing with angry texts from her saying really vile things about Ray and how he had been rude to Anne. *Don't tell me you're siding with that man and his major sulking when we've protected him all these years every time the men in our family have slagged him off*, she wrote. I couldn't believe what I was reading.

The next thing I knew I had Auntie Theresa on the line. 'I'm phoning about this row that Ray and Anne have had,' she said. 'I don't want to get involved but if what Anne says is true then Ray is right out of order.'

'So you are involved,' I said.

'No.'

'Yes, you are,' I snapped back. 'But you haven't heard his side, have you?'

Poor Ray had always felt like a bit of a spare part at Nolan family gatherings. He'd say he had the feeling that the other men weren't all that welcoming and didn't want him to be part of the gang. For years I'd told him he was imagining it. Now it appeared to be true!

As the journey home continued, so did the texts – each more vile than the last. In the end I texted back, *Please stop this now, it's getting out of hand.* But Denise wouldn't let it go. She was insisting I'd never liked her and that I'd upset her at a do we'd been to. When she told me which it was I almost laughed. It had happened fifteen years earlier! The more texts she sent, the more upset Ray and I became. By the time we reached home Ray was shaking with anger. I've rarely seen him more upset. For him it was confirmation that he was the outsider he'd always suspected.

For the next few days he was in a terrible state. He couldn't sleep, he lost his appetite, and he kept replaying the argument with Anne around and around in his head. He was so devastated I thought he was going to have a nervous breakdown.

'I've got to tell them my side of the story,' he told me one night, when we were lying in bed.

'Do you really think that's such a good idea?' I asked. 'You know what they've been like – it may just make things worse.'

'I've got to, Col,' he said. 'It feels like I can't let it rest until I've had my say.'

Ray wrote every member of the family a long letter, explaining what had happened. He said that he was willing to meet Denise and Anne to talk things through and he hand-delivered each letter. Well, he didn't get a single response. I know now that the others were trying not to get involved, but by staying silent they were doing just that. Poor Ray was more distressed than ever.

Mum and Dad had raised us girls and our two brothers as a tight family unit. I can still hear them now telling us that the Nolans were never wrong. 'Blood is thicker than water,' they'd say, and they'd insist that we stuck together. It was the Nolans against the world. It was Ray who kind of made me stick up for myself. I can be very easily intimidated, but he made me believe it was OK to say no. He made me stand up to Shane, to my family . . . and it's the first time I'd ever stood up to anyone and said, 'You're wrong.' Because we Nolans are never wrong. Over the years 'outsiders' – our brothers- and sisters-in-law – had fallen foul of this family rule and, as a result, been isolated for a while. I was determined it wasn't going to happen to Ray. If I'd believed he was wrong and needed to apologize to Anne I'd have asked him to do it. But this time I knew it wasn't his fault. I had to defend him because nobody else in the family was going to.

The feud continued and created huge problems for us, especially around the time of our wedding in 2007. Ray was jittery and said he didn't know if he could go through with it. 'I just can't marry into a family where everyone hates me and thinks I'm trying to split them up,' he'd say.

'You're not marrying them, you're marrying me!' I'd tell him.

So it was off, then on, then off again. There were times when I thought our relationship wouldn't survive but, in the end, the wedding went ahead – without Anne and Denise, which was sad. Some awful things had been said but it was still hard enjoying one of the most important days of my life knowing that two of my sisters weren't there to share it with me.

So, fast forward two years and here we were, being offered a comeback tour, but sadly without Anne. I didn't need a crystal ball to know how much trouble it was going to cause. And I was right.

Denise had left the Nolans pretty early on. She'd never felt comfortable in the band, even though she's got a really great voice. So for her to be part of the tour was never an option. But Anne had very much been part of the line-up and she was absolutely furious to be left out now.

With Anne and I not really speaking, it was left to Linda, Maureen and Bernie to do their best to explain to her that the decision had been Universal's.

'It's out of our hands, Anne,' Maureen told her. 'We've begged them to reconsider but it's not going to happen.'

'You should be telling them you won't do it without me,' she argued.

I can only imagine now that Anne was too upset by the news to think straight. At that stage she was more sad than angry and I couldn't really blame her. I'd done my best, too. Right at the start I'd told Universal that I could work with Anne – even though we'd fallen out there was no way I was going to spoil things for my big sister – and asked them to include her but they wouldn't agree. She's never believed that and perhaps, if I had been in her shoes, I wouldn't either. But it's God's honest truth.

Once again Denise became involved and this time she accused Linda of being a Judas. It had been only two years since poor Linda had lost her husband to cancer and then had to fight her own battle with the disease. She and Brian had been together 24/7 for twenty-eight years and she was lost without him. She'd told me once that the Nolans had always been his favourite band and he'd always hoped that one day we would get back together. Now it was actually going to happen and it was something for her to get out of bed for each morning. To ask her to give up this chance was too cruel.

With Linda clearly not on their side, Denise and Anne said that Maureen and Bernie should pull out of the tour and force Universal to reconsider. But Universal just weren't budging. In fact, one boss there said they were so determined the tour go ahead that we would carry on without them! Denise and Anne began bombarding the others with texts. Maureen, always the peacemaker, would be in tears and Bernie would want to kill them.

'There must be a way round all this,' Maureen would say. 'Is the tour really worth tearing the family apart over?'

'There's no talking to them,' Bernie would chip in. 'The texts I've been getting are just unforgivable.'

Welcome to my world, I'd think. Now you can see I haven't been exaggerating all these years.

I think we all felt hurt and upset, and possibly quite guilty, but it was such a fantastic opportunity that we couldn't afford to say no. We're far from millionaires and there were mortgages to pay and mouths to feed. I hope that if I'd been in Anne's shoes I would have understood. I'd have said, 'Christ, I'm angry, but you can't turn down such an amazing offer.' Then I'd have collected what was left of my dignity and bought my ticket so that I could stand in the front row and cheer them on. But she couldn't do it. The texts continued, even after the tour had kicked off. *I've got no sisters now*, she wrote. It was an awful thing for her to say but by now the damage was done. Too many other unpleasant things had been said, and in the end we stopped responding to the messages. In a way, the anger we felt made it easier just to get on with it. And once we'd made that decision, nothing and nobody was going to ruin the tour for us.

First we had to record a CD of the songs from our set at a studio in Manchester. In the eighties we'd spend an entire day putting down a single track but times had moved on and now we were expected to record four songs in every session. It was exhausting but exciting!

We'd chosen the kind of songs that we knew would make women feel empowered. Songs like 'I Will Survive', 'It's Raining Men' and some of our own hits, like 'Attention To Me' and, of course, 'I'm In The Mood For Dancing'. Every number was a real party favourite and just right for our stage of life. The songs were also perfect for the fans who came to see us – women in their forties and fifties hell bent on having a great night out.

Then we had to film our DVD, record an advertisement for it and keep to a whirlwind promotional schedule to let everyone know about the show. I was used to being on the likes of *This Morning* and *Loose Women* but to be sitting on TV sofas alongside my sisters was wonderful. Newspapers, magazines and radio stations all wanted to cover the tour and we'd travel from interview to interview, happy to give it the big build-up.

We were amazed at what a major event it was turning out to be. Universal had arranged for Kim Gavin to choreograph our dance routines. Kim's amazing. He was responsible for the choreography for the Take That tour and went on to become the creative director for the 2012 Olympics closing ceremony, so we were in good hands. My God, it was a long way from those early days when we'd make up dance moves in our parents' front room in Blackpool. Now we'd get to rehearsals and the producer would say, 'So this is where the eight male dancers come in.'

We were, like, 'Sorry? Eight male dancers, you say? Well, if we must!' And we'd get eight of the most gorgeous men with us on stage, dancing around us as if we were the most glamorous creatures on earth.

Then there was the catering. When we were touring in the eighties we'd have to nip out to McDonald's for a burger. We were lucky if anyone made us a cup of tea! Now it felt like we were in the lap of luxury. We'd have beautiful costumes, clean laundered undies and fabulous food waiting for us when we arrived at the arena. Then top hair and makeup artists would get to work on us to transform us for our stage appearance. There were five, six, seven changes of clothes, and people couldn't do enough for us – it was fabulous.

The best bit, though, was that, despite the rows with Denise and Anne, the tour had become a true family affair. My Ray was to be part of our band and play guitar, as was Bernie's husband Steve, who played drums. My boys Shane Junior and Jake had been offered an amazing break as the support act and even Ciara, to her absolute delight, was going to be travelling with us. I was worried because I'd dreaded having to leave her. How can you say to a child, 'Well, your father, your two brothers and I are going off on tour – see you in a month!' You just couldn't. Luckily, she was at a brilliant school where the head agreed to her having four weeks off. Some schools would have made a massive fuss but her teachers agreed it was an experience she shouldn't miss. They provided her with schoolwork and every day she'd sit poring over her books on the tour bus. By the time she returned she wasn't a single day behind her classmates.

Before we went on the road, the entire set was put up in a studio at Elstree so that we could run through a dress rehearsal in front of an invited audience of family and friends. We'd rehearsed so much in the run-up that we were able to go straight through all of our numbers without a break. It felt amazing to be performing at last in front of a proper live audience with my sisters by my side. When we finished, the crowd went wild and gave us just a taste of what was to come.

'Oh, my God! That was absolutely amazing,' I said, as we gave our final bow and blew kisses to our loved ones. 'I just can't wait to do it for real now!'

October soon rolled around and the first night was

almost upon us. We'd been staying together in a hotel and were nattering away in one of the bedrooms with *News at 10* on the TV in the background. Suddenly, through the excited chatter, we heard, 'And finally . . . after thirty years away, the Nolans are back and in the mood for dancing!' I can't tell you what that felt like. The four of us girls were whooping and jumping up and down on the beds, screaming. It was just like being in a wonderful dream.

Then we started to get really nervous. Universal had booked the country's biggest venues for the tour, including some massive arenas. Back in the eighties when we were in the Top 10, there didn't seem to be that many big arenas out there and I couldn't remember ever having filled such a large venue. We'd never experienced standing on a massive stage in front of thousands of people.

'Oh, my God, what if no one comes?' I whispered to Maureen one night, when we were in our hotel room. 'We might get on stage and find ourselves singing to empty seats.'

'Shut up, Col,' she said. 'Don't start saying things like that!'

We needn't have worried. Neil told me that the concert tickets were selling quickly, and by the time we opened on 11 October at Nottingham's Royal Concert Hall we already knew that every seat in the house would be taken.

If we were nervous you can imagine how Shane Junior and Jake felt opening the show for us. My heart went out to my boys. They weren't even a double act, just two brothers who sang together from time to time. Someone from Universal had heard them doing a few songs at my wedding and thought it would be a nice idea to offer them the support slot. Shane had been working as a Pontin's Blue Coat – like his dad before him – so he had some experience of performing and Jake had studied at the famous Sylvia Young Theatre School in London, but neither of them had done anything on this scale before. Shane was twenty-one and Jake just seventeen but, despite their tender ages, they both said yes the moment they were asked.

'What do you mean, yes?' I said, when they told me. 'What on earth are you going to do?'

'Erm, we're not sure, really,' said Shane, sheepishly. 'It just seemed like a good idea at the time!'

In the end, Ray and I helped them out. We worked together choosing songs and Ray recorded some backing tracks with them. Despite their inexperience, I had to admit they sounded good together. Luckily they had no idea what it was going to be like having to perform in front of so many people so they seemed confident right up to the time when they had to take to the stage.

That opening night in Nottingham I had terrible first-night nerves. But the thought of my kids walking on stage made me feel physically sick. I was dying inside. Their aunties had warned the boys that traditionally the support can find itself performing to half-empty theatres because often people only turn up to see the main act. 'You'll get polite applause but don't take that as a knock-back,' said Linda. 'It's a great break, whatever happens.'

Shane was pretending not to be bothered. He gives the impression that nothing frightens him but as his mum I know that's not true. Poor Jake, on the other hand, was sick with nerves. He actually looked grey. 'That's fine,' he replied bravely to Linda. 'You don't need to worry. That's what we're expecting.'

Just before their names were announced he suddenly grabbed hold of me. 'I'm going to be sick,' he said. By now he was an interesting shade of green.

My poor baby! I held his shoulders and stroked his hair. I was going to have to be tough for him. 'No, you're not, Jake,' I said. 'Just shut up and get out there!' I gave him a gentle shove and went to wait in my dressing room with the rest of the girls. I could hear the pre-recorded intro I'd done for them, then there was a second's silence before the place went mad. An almighty roar went up – the crowd loved them!

The boys started with Take That's 'Greatest Day' and then went into a bit of Michael Jackson. With every song we could hear the audience getting louder and louder, and it was clear that people had come early because they hadn't wanted to miss seeing Shane and Jake. Bernie, Linda, Maureen and I looked at each other in disbelief. Could it be that a second generation of singing Nolans was about to make the big-time? Each one of us was crying, we were so proud of them. By the time they got to their last number, the Robbie

Williams version of 'Me And My Shadow', we were starting to worry they were going down a bit too well! They were only meant to be the support and were in danger of outshining us completely!

I went to wait for them in the wings and found myself standing next to the stage manager. 'I've been here thirty years and that's the best reaction to a support I've ever heard,' he said.

I thought I would burst with pride. 'They take after their mother,' I joked. But, actually, they needed to come off while the going was good!

'Come off now,' I was shouting to them, from the wings. 'Seriously, come off now!' And the next thing they were taking their bows and leaping off stage, whooping with delight.

'Oh, my God,' screamed Jake, his cheeks now back to their usual rosy colour. 'That was so fantastic, I didn't want it to end!'

Shane swept me off my feet and kissed me. 'Amazing!' he said.

'Remember that feeling,' I said, hugging Jake and giving Shane's hair a ruffle. 'Just in case it's a one-off.' But it wasn't. Every night the crowd went bananas for them and I couldn't have been more delighted.

Then it was our turn. The massive set had taken hours to put up and was now waiting for the show to kick off. Huge sparkly sliding doors with 'The Nolans' emblazoned across them stood on top of a platform. The idea was that the eight (gorgeous) male dancers would come on and do their bit, the spotlight would hit the screen and the doors would slide open to reveal the four of us standing with our backs to the audience. We'd turn around and launch into our first song – Bonnie Tyler's 'Holding Out For A Hero'.

As we waited behind the closed doors I looked at Bernie, Maureen and Linda and wondered if they were as terrified as I was. Oh, Lord Jesus, I remember thinking. Please, God, let it be OK. We held each other's hot, trembling hands and wished each other good luck, then heard our cue. The doors slid open and there was such a roar that I honestly thought one of the dancers had fallen over or that Coldplay had walked on.

I heard one of us – it may even have been me – say, 'Fucking hell.' And then we turned around and the crowd leaped to their feet to start dancing. They stayed on their feet after that first song, and it was like that for the whole tour, every single night.

It felt amazing being back on stage with my sisters. We'd chosen real diva numbers and mixed our old hits in with some newer covers. As well as singing together we all had solos – I sang Alesha Dixon's 'The Boy Does Nothing', Linda sang Duffy's 'Mercy', Maureen did 'Valerie' by The Zutons and Bernie sang Pink's 'So What'. With so many hours of rehearsal behind us we belted out those songs with gusto. It really was the best feeling in the world.

Every few numbers we'd do a costume change, switching from one amazing outfit to the next. The finale of the show could only ever have been one song. So, as the first strains of 'I'm In The Mood For Dancing' were heard, we had to dash backstage to get into our fabulous black spangly catsuits. As the music played we could hear the audience singing the song ahead of us. By the time we got back on stage to sing the song ourselves the noise was off the scale. It felt so good to see everyone having as much fun as we were.

We were all on such a wave of euphoria afterwards that we didn't want the night to end. Most of the family had tickets for the opening night and afterwards they rushed backstage to congratulate us.

'I didn't know what to expect but that was just fabulous,' said my brother, Brian. It meant a lot. I know that my family will always tell me the truth and they kept coming to see us again and again throughout the tour. I guess he must have meant it!

And so the tour went on. From Nottingham to Manchester, Blackpool to Liverpool, each night brought a new city and another evening of exhilaration – and not only for us. The music would start and you could almost hear the audience saying as one, 'I love this song!' The latter part of 2009 was really miserable and people were fed up with the credit crunch. It seemed like we had chosen just the right time to try to bring a little fun back into the lives of the nation.

Of course, with Ciara and the rest of the family in tow, I'd often have to switch quickly back into mum mode. One night she was feeling ill and came into our hotel room to sleep with Ray and me. She spent half the night throwing up into the loo and was so tired and poorly I actually found her asleep on the bathroom floor wrapped around the toilet. It made me think how surreal the whole thing was. One moment I was on stage with people cheering and screaming for me, the next I was holding my child's hair back while she vomited.

Whatever bug Ciara had caught soon did its worst to the rest of us. The night after, halfway through a song, Ray had to run off stage to projectile vomit in the wings.

A few hours later I was standing at the stage door signing autographs. One of the theatre staff told me that a lady in a wheelchair was waiting at the top of some stairs. 'She's a massive fan but she can't get down to you,' they said.

'Tell her I'll be up as soon as I can,' I said, and carried on signing a few more autographs before making my way up the stairs to find her. The poor lady must have been waiting an hour and a half. It was October and chilly and it meant a lot to me that she had waited so patiently.

'Oh, Coleen, it's lovely to meet you. I'm such a fan,' she said, when I finally reached her.

I took her hand, looked into her eyes and said, 'I'm going to be sick!' I was thinking, I can't be sick over a lady in a wheelchair who's been waiting for me for an hour and a half, so I ran away to find a more discreet place. Whoever you are, lovely lady in the wheelchair, if you're reading this book, I am so, so sorry!

When the tour manager saw how unwell I was he wouldn't let me on the bus because he was worried I would spread my bug around everyone else. He didn't want the other three Nolans and the rest of the band having to dash off stage to be ill. He offered to get a taxi with me and there I was, throwing up into a bin bag all the way to the next venue. I was wailing, 'I don't know you well enough to share my vomit!' God knows what the cab driver was thinking.

So, that was the glamorous life on tour with the Nolans! It had its moments but there were times when I was definitely put in my place. Take, for instance, the reception Ray got from the fans. If anything was to remind me of the power of *Loose Women* it was the huge cheer that went up every night when it was time for the band to be introduced and Ray took his bow. I'd been laughing about old Chicken Legs on *Loose Women* for ten years and the women in the audience felt like they knew him. We'd introduce him and up would go a massive cheer. Then they'd all stamp their feet and they'd be chanting, 'Ray! Ray! Ray!' In the end we had to tell them to shut up! The first night it happened Ray was so shocked. He's actually quite shy and so he was mortified to find himself the centre of attention. But it happened every night and he eventually got used to it.

Those lovely women had such a good time at the concerts. They'd arrive with a crowd of mates, all dressed up in feather boas, high heels and party outfits, usually having had a few drinks and a good laugh. I don't know who was having the best time – them or us!

When Universal first suggested the tour we were worried we might be a bit past it. I was the youngest and in my mid-forties and Maureen, the eldest, in her mid-fifties. We asked ourselves if anyone would pay to see us dancing around on stage in tight-fitting outfits with raunchy young men.

'That lad dancing with me is young enough to be my son,' Maureen would laugh.

But we needn't have worried. Most of the audience were of a similar age and it was just so refreshing to see them celebrating sexy mature women.

The clear message was that for a few hours each night it really didn't matter how old you were, what shape you were in or what you did. It didn't matter if you were a mum, a housewife or a high-flying career woman. The important lesson was clear: do whatever you want in life. It was so empowering.

Over the years we'd all seen younger acts and bands turning up with their entourage and moaning about their lot. They'd demand riders like vintage champagne or special tea or fresh flowers and you'd think, Jeez, you don't know how lucky you are to have so much help and support, with your in-ears and radio mics and stylists. Now we had all that stuff too – although we weren't about to start demanding champagne and roses. Nevertheless there was no way we were going to take it for granted. We lapped it up and shared our enthusiasm with the fantastic women who had come to see us. Like them we were survivors – the theme of the show – and we were in it together.

Every night I was sad, knowing that we were one show closer to the end. But living out of a suitcase was starting to take its toll. Ray, Ciara, Shane, Jake and I had all this luggage and each morning, even though I had been dancing on stage for two or three hours the previous evening, I would be trying to make sure everyone had packed their bags and not left anything behind. There were times when I thought, I'm getting too old for this now.

But it was the only part of the tour that I didn't enjoy and in some ways I wish it had gone on for longer. If I could have had a six-month break – gone home, washed my undies, had a bit of real life – then returned to the road and done it again I would have jumped at the chance. We'd always said we didn't want to tour unless we could do it properly, and Universal certainly let us do that.

The last night of the tour was in Belfast, just before Christmas. We were all exhausted but determined to put on one more great show. As ever the audience was fantastic and I think we all knew it was likely to be the last time we would sing together on such a spectacular level. Everything seemed even more special that night. The atmosphere was electric, the music sounded amazing and the four of us were full of adrenalin.

When the last few notes of 'I'm In The Mood' rang out we held each other's hands and took our final bow. None of us wanted to come off stage that night. We kept walking towards the wings and then one of us would drag the others back to sing yet another encore.

I can remember looking at Bernie, thinking, My God, how astonishing is her voice? She was always ambitious. For her it was all about the singing and, apart from being a mum, it was all she had ever wanted to do. It was what made her tick and she just loved that tour. She was in her element. I thank God that the stage show was recorded and that Universal released a live DVD because now we have it for ever. To Shane, Jake, Ciara and Erin, it's an amazing thing to have.

I never get tired of watching it. When I feel like cheering myself up I put it on and curl up on the sofa. There we are, dancing with our gorgeous young men, strutting our stuff and socking it to the rest of the world. And I think, Oh, my God. That really was the best time of our lives.

# Chapter Three

In April 2010, something happened at home that took my mind off work entirely, but not in a good way. After his success being part of the Nolans' tour band, Ray got a job playing guitar for Rick Astley on the Peter Kay tour and it turned out to be a massive wake-up call for my marriage.

Of course I was dead chuffed for him because he lives for music and, apart from our show, it was the first job he'd had in a long time. When I met Ray he was playing guitar in a show called Legends – a night of Elvis, Robbie Williams and Elton John tribute acts – which was popular at the time in Blackpool. He'd toured with the band doing corporate events all over the world, including parties for Ivana Trump, famous footballers and the like. Since we'd been married I'd been the main breadwinner and I knew that Ray had missed being involved in the business. I've been out with a lot of musicians and I'd learned that performing is their passion. It's no different with Ray. I've always known that I'd only ever come second to his flipping guitar. Of course, these days I'm third in line: it's his guitar, then Ciara, then me. That's absolutely fine. I've learned to live with it!

He'd loved being part of the Nolans' tour band but

I knew he was plagued by this thought: I wouldn't have done it if I hadn't been married to Coleen. Ray's always been like that – so unconfident in his own abilities when in fact he's a really good musician. When we finished touring, he hadn't expected anything else like it to come along but somebody saw him playing and offered him the Rick Astley job. For him to get such a great gig on his own merits was a real shot in the arm. He was ecstatic at being right back into proper music mode and knowing that somebody – apart from his wife and sisters-in-law – thought he was good at what he did.

'See? What did I tell you, Ray?' I said, after he'd heard the news. 'There's loads of other people out there who need a good guitarist.'

But there was a problem. I'd had Ray to myself for seven years up until that point and, although he was only a few miles away at the Manchester Evening News Arena and was home every night, it scared me that he was loving it so much. It sounds really selfish to admit that now, but that was how I felt. Of course, it didn't help that he became totally wrapped up in it. All he wanted to talk about was the bloody show – it was great to see him with a new lease on life but it was a struggle for me. I'd always had him on hand to talk to, he was my constant, and now even when he was home it was as if he wasn't listening to a word I said.

'Er, Ray, can you run Ciara over to the stables?' I'd ask him, as I was dashing around trying to organize the shopping and the washing and my own TV work schedule. Nothing. His blond head was bowed over his beloved guitar and he was lost in his own little world. 'Bloody hell, Earth to Planet Ray!' I'd shout, chucking a sofa cushion in his direction.

Yes, overall I was delighted for him and, yes, it was wonderful to see him being so passionate about something. But the situation was starting to stir up uncomfortable feelings from my time with Shane, feelings that I thought I'd buried long ago. Up until that moment, I don't think I'd ever realized quite how much I was still affected by what had happened with my ex-husband. You assume a broken heart is mended, but apparently the scars still twinge every now and again.

Suddenly Ray was involved with all these exciting people I didn't know, which was exactly what had happened when things started to go wrong first time around with Shane. I adore Ray and I'm completely over Shane, but sometimes the legacy of a marriage break-up can still affect you many years after the divorce. The end of a marriage is one of the most traumatic things you can go through in life and the scars can run deep. Even though I hardly ever gave my first marriage a second thought, it had left deep-seated feelings that I didn't know I had, and I think it's worth explaining some of the backstory briefly here.

Back in 1996, Shane had gone to Manchester to work on *Grease*, leaving me at our home in London with toddlers Shane Junior and Jake. He was having the time of his life, meeting all these new people and lapping up attention from screaming girls in the audience. Women have always loved Shane Richie and I was constantly hearing rumours that he was seeing this one or that. Once, I even saw a photograph of him with his arms around a very pretty girl – and she didn't look as if she was merely asking for an autograph. It was actually five-year-old Jake who found it. He'd been playing in the basement when he came upstairs holding some photos.

'Mum, who is this lady with Daddy?' he asked. Some sixth sense told me the picture spelled trouble. When I looked at it I felt sick. The girl was giggling and Shane was closing in as if he was about to kiss her.

'It's just a friend of Daddy's,' I reassured Jake. 'Let me put them somewhere safe for him.'

The girl in the picture turned out to be Claire – who was to figure large in our lives – but at the time Shane said she was a friend of one of the dancers in *Grease*. That's what he told me anyway. My old sixth sense told me he was lying.

Even when he wasn't working away, Shane would spend hours out of the house. There were no explanations, no apologies. One night, when my self-esteem was at its lowest, I begged him not to leave me alone for yet another night. 'Oh, give it a rest, Col,' he snapped coldly at me. I felt so worthless that I slumped to the floor and broke my heart crying. Shane merely stepped over me on his way out.

It wasn't long after that I discovered the true reason behind his mystery trips out. He was seeing Claire. If

I'd been stronger, more confident, I might have fought her for him but Shane had crushed the Coleen Nolan I'd once been. When I caught him red-handed that was that – the end of our marriage.

So, when Ray came home and started chatting about the show and all these exciting people he'd met, the same old fear just hit me. In particular, he'd made friends with two young backing singers and he talked about them a lot. It was all 'Scarlet said that and Amy said this and Scarlet looked fab last night.' I was thinking, If I hear how amazing sodding Scarlet and Amy are one more time I'll go over there and punch their bloody lights out!

The more I heard about those two girls the more the old insecurities and fears I'd had over Shane's cheating came to the surface. It gave me such a jolt. I really thought I'd got over all of that long ago, but it slapped me right in the face completely unexpectedly. Up until now, good old solid Ray had always seemed the perfect antidote to someone as unreliable and ultra-confident as Shane. Bless him, Ray had never given me a single reason to doubt him. This was the first time anything like this had happened in my marriage and I immediately panicked and thought, Oh, God, it's all going to go wrong again.

I take my job as a newspaper agony aunt very ser-iously, and really think through the advice I give people. In my responses I'm always talking about the import-ance of communication. Those couples who don't thrash out their problems usually find it impossible to resolve matters in any meaningful way. What's the old saying? It's good to talk. So, did I take my own advice? Of course not! I tried loads of times to sit down with Ray and talk things through, but he isn't a great talker at the best of times. When I think back now we could have saved ourselves a whole heap of heartache if we had only sat up through the night and bashed it out between us as soon as our problems arose. I guess these things are always easier in hindsight!

If only Ray had just put his arms around me and said, 'Don't be paranoid, Col, because I'm not Shane and everything's absolutely fine. I'm just loving what I'm doing.' But he didn't. Instead he got angry with me for being constantly suspicious and not understanding how he felt. From his point of view, he was coming home to this insecure, crying wife, whom he'd loyally supported for seven years but who was doing everything in her power to ruin things for him.

'What time did you come to bed last night?' I'd ask.

'Give it a rest, will you?' he'd grunt.

'By the way, you could have bought some bread and milk yesterday afternoon before you went out. Ciara and I had to go to the supermarket last night after the stables,' I'd nag. 'Were you too keen to get to your mates in Manchester and forget us?'

Often I knew I'd gone too far. 'For Christ's sake, Col,' he would roar. 'I've been working all night and I'm knackered.'

He was angry and bad-tempered, which made me feel incredibly guilty and scared. I hated hearing myself sound so weak and whiny and I worried I'd end up pushing him away for good. A lot of the time I had two voices in my head – like an angel and a devil – which seemed to be permanently at war. They went something like this:

'All I'm asking for is a bit of reassurance and he's not bloody giving it to me.'

'Yes, but he's remembering all the times you've been away and he's been left at home with the kids.'

'Is that a reason to be so goddamn angry all the time?'

'Well, perhaps if you didn't constantly compare him to your first (cheating) husband he wouldn't be!'

It couldn't go on and it wasn't long before I had a proper, very public meltdown. I'd been crying for days because I'd convinced myself that my second marriage was about to go belly-up. I thought Ray didn't care and wanted his freedom so he could pursue his career. After so long in the public eye I'm normally pretty good at hiding my feelings, but one day at *Loose Women* I found myself losing the plot. I was sitting in the morning meeting with the girls and the editors and we were discussing the topics on the show that day, one of which was 'If your relationship is in trouble, how easy do you find it to talk about?' Instantly I felt this lump rising in my throat because I'd been bottling up my emotions and fears for days – I hadn't been able to tell any of my friends or my sisters how I was feeling. I jumped up from my seat and literally ran out of the meeting, mumbling something like 'Sorry, I've got to go,' between sobs. When I got outside the floodgates opened and I couldn't stop crying.

I called Neil straight away and told him I wasn't up to doing the show that day. Now, that's not like me, I'm generally not one to let anyone down or cause a fuss, so he knew I was serious. I think he was shocked because he'd never heard me so upset before, so he jumped in a cab and was there in ten minutes, bless him. Our editor, Emily, came outside, too, to find out what all the drama was about.

'Emily, is there anyone we can get in to cover for Coleen on the show today because she can't stop crying?' Neil asked, worried.

'Look, if I could get someone in to cover I absolutely would, but it's too late now. We won't do that topic, though,' she reassured me.

'You know what, Emily? Right now you could do a topic about Pinky and Perky and I'd still cry,' I sniffed.

As it turned out, we didn't have any option and I had to do *Loose Women*. The show must go on and all that. I'm pretty sure the viewers would never have guessed that, just hours ago, I was breaking my heart crying. But, still, inside I felt desperately sad and worried. Sherrie Hewson, Jane McDonald and Andrea McLean were on the panel that day and I warned them not to be nice to me or even to look at me sympathetically as I was liable to burst into tears!

That afternoon, after the show had finished, I caught the train home. The moment we pulled out of Euston I began to cry and I carried on all the way from London to Wilmslow. Luckily it was a quiet train and nobody saw me sobbing into my cup of milky takeaway tea. I pulled out my phone and texted Ray on the way: *I've been crying all day. I even cried in the meeting. I can't bear this. It probably is me, but you need to help me through it.* Then I called Shane Junior and asked him to pick up Ciara from school and take her out somewhere because I didn't want her to see me so upset. I felt sure I'd get a text from Ray before the end of the journey but my phone stayed quiet.

When I arrived home, I wasn't sure whether Ray would be there. I was hoping he'd have registered the pain in my text and be waiting for me, ready to sort the whole thing out. My absolute dread was that I'd discover an empty house.

I paid the taxi driver and approached the front door. As I walked up the drive, the house looked ominously dark. I fished in my handbag and found my keys. Come on, Ray, I said to myself. Be in, please. I put my key in the door and stepped into the hallway. To my joy, I saw his coat on the hook and knew that he was there. But my relief was short-lived. As soon as I saw his face I knew there was little chance we'd be having that big conversation I'd hoped for. He didn't smile or make any move to kiss me, he just seemed so cold. I thought then that we were done for. For a professional musician, getting to play to a packed-out arena like the MEN is like discovering the Holy Grail. It was obvious he resented me spoiling things for him.

I put my bags down and walked into the kitchen to make a pot of tea. 'Can't we just talk about this, please?'

I said, as I filled the kettle with water. 'It's been driving me mad all day.'

Ray was sitting in the living room, staring at the television. A nature programme was on but I could tell he wasn't watching it. His hands were shoved deep into his jeans pockets and his body was stiff, as if rage was coursing through his veins. I made him a cup of tea and took it over to him. He stared straight ahead at the TV and ignored me.

'Please can we switch the telly off and have a conversation?' I begged. 'Ray?'

He dragged his eyes from the screen to me and the look on his face was dreadful. I'd never seen him so distant. He was being so cold it shook me. 'I'm actually doing something I never thought I'd do again in my life, and I certainly didn't think I'd be doing it in my fifties,' he said. 'It's as if you wished I hadn't been given the job.'

'Honest, Ray, I'm happy for you,' I promised him. 'I just feel that we're not spending time together. I worry you're pulling away from me, and it's making me feel insecure. I just need to know that everything is OK between us.'

But my assurances fell on deaf ears. Ray didn't even wait for his cup of tea, just turned his back and went into his office to mess around on his guitar. I watched him leave and felt devastated. Didn't he want to try to sort things out? Our relationship was usually so close and tender, but at that point it felt like we were miles apart. It was obvious to me that Ray wasn't ready to talk and that things weren't going to resolve themselves that day. Ray doesn't find it easy to express his emotions, so once again he just kind of backed off.

I walked back to the kitchen, sat at the table and cried my eyes out. I felt like I'd been punched. I had told him how terrible I felt and he was just walking away from me. I stared at the clock on the kitchen wall and thought about all the texts that had gone unanswered, all the nights I'd sat at home feeling lonely and miserable. I'd had enough. As he was leaving to go to Manchester later that afternoon, I shouted after him, 'I don't want you to come back tonight.' We've all done it. Any woman will know that what I really wanted was for him to turn around and say, 'Well, I am coming back because I want to be with you.' I was trying to shock him out of it. But instead he just said, 'Fine,' and slammed the door on his way out. I went back to the kitchen and sobbed again.

I sat in the empty house and waited for him to text or call but he didn't contact me and I was too upset to get in touch with him. We'd never rowed like that and it felt really serious. The deafening silence between us made me feel a million times worse than I had before. By the time Shane and Ciara came home I had dried my tears and put on a bit of makeup to hide my distress but I don't think I was fooling anyone.

'Are you OK, Mum?' Ciara asked, putting her arms around my neck and giving me a cuddle.

'Yes, love, don't worry,' I told her.

It felt very strange lying alone in our big bed that

night. In a way I was used to it. Ray's exciting new job meant he didn't get home until late but that night, knowing he was unlikely to return at all, I felt very sad and lonely. The next morning I fixed a smile on my face and tried not to let Ciara see that I was upset. Shane Junior was an angel and offered to take her to school. He obviously knew by now there was a problem but he sensibly didn't press me for details.

Around mid-morning Ray sent a text telling me he would have to come home to pick up some of his things.

*How are you?* I texted back.

*I'm pissed off!* came the reply. About an hour later I heard his key in the door and then the sound of his footsteps as he ran up the stairs to our bedroom. I followed him, dreading the scene, and found him throwing clothes into a suitcase lying open on our bed.

'What do you want to do?' I asked, terrified of hearing his answer.

He stopped tossing jeans and shirts into the case and looked at me. 'I want to come home, Coleen,' he replied.

I was so relieved.

'Fine, just come home, then,' I said. I knew we had to discuss things properly. Perhaps this brief moment of madness between us would be enough to shock us into talking honestly to one another. But Ray needed to get back to work and our talk would have to wait. It was Friday so I arranged for Ciara to have a sleepover at her best friend's house, then sat up to wait for Ray to get home from work. I must have drunk a million cups of tea and smoked a thousand cigarettes that night but there was no point going to bed. I couldn't have slept if I'd tried.

I hate having big shouting matches. In a family as large and noisy as mine I'm used to people raising their voices but I've always been the Nolan sister who tries to avoid trouble and keep the peace. Even during my first marriage to Shane, with things so bad between us, we rarely screamed at one another. But this was different. As soon as Ray walked through the door it was as if the tension that had been building up over the past few weeks suddenly came to a head and burst. We ended up letting go and having the biggest row of our lives.

I was lying in the dark on the sofa with a blanket over me when he flicked on the light. The brightness hurt my eyes but I could see immediately that he had a face like thunder.

'You should have gone to bed. This can wait for the morning,' he said.

But I'd had enough waiting. 'It can't, Ray,' I told him. 'I'm not prepared to be treated like this again.'

'Treated like what?' His voice was rising now. 'All I've ever done is support you and Ciara and now I'm working hard, doing something I love, and you won't stop moaning.'

'I don't care how much you love it! You're supposed to love me!' By now I was shouting, too.

'Jesus, Col, you know I love you!' Ray yelled.

'That's what Shane said and look what happened!'

Ray's face was scarlet. 'I'm not Shane Richie!'

'Well, don't fucking act like him, then!'

To be honest, I absolutely lost it and was screaming the place down because the kids weren't at home, but it felt good. I never do that kind of thing and I needed to just get it all out and to clear the air.

In some respects I suppose it was the start of me really questioning our relationship because I didn't like the way Ray had reacted. It wasn't just my insecurity that was to blame, it was his behaviour, too. Whatever it was that was eating away at him, he just couldn't give me the reassurance I was desperate for. When I needed a hug most he couldn't give me one, and that really upset me.

The thing is, Ray and I are very different people, which is what makes us great together, but it's also what causes angst. We're poles apart when it comes to how we view relationships. I'm a very tactile kind of person. I'm romantic and I don't have an issue with saying, 'I love you.' I like to go out for dinner and away for weekends. Don't get me wrong, I don't want bunches of flowers and boxes of chocolates all the time, but I love a hug or a nice text once in a while.

Ray, on the other hand, is the absolute opposite. He's a typical gruff Yorkshireman, who doesn't need any of that stuff and, what's more, he doesn't understand why anyone else would need it either. Sometimes I can deal with that and sometimes I can't. I've said to him in the past, 'All it takes, Ray, is for you to pass me in the kitchen and give me a hug for no reason. For no reason at all! And that will make me happy for the next month.'

If only men knew how easy it is to make a woman – at least, this woman – happy. It's not rocket science.

In the end it took something really shocking like that row to make us both come to our senses. Some terrible things were said that night but, thankfully, we ended it in each other's arms, with Ray giving me the reassurance I'd been looking for.

'I'm sorry, Nolan Face,' he told me, using his old nickname for me for the first time in ages.

'Me too,' I whispered, leaning my head on his shoulder.

After that, things began to calm down and I did what I should have done in the first place: I went with Ray to work to meet some of the people he was spending time with. The show was amazing. Peter Kay was hilarious and Rick Astley sounded great. It was so lovely to see Ray in the band, guitar in hand, doing what he loved. He looked so comfortable and I could see why it made him so happy. After the show I finally got to meet Scarlet and Amy – and they couldn't have been nicer. In fact, we clicked right away and I see them all the time now: they've actually become good mates. Yes, they're both young and gorgeous but, even so, they're flattered that I thought Ray fancied them!

'Coleen, you have to know that he just goes on about you all the time!' Amy giggled.

I wish I could say that was the end of the story and

that we lived happily ever after, but life's not really like that, is it? By this stage I'd stopped imagining that Ray was having a torrid affair, but he was still infuriating me. Something about him was driving me crazy and leading to constant rows. But writing this book has been therapeutic and, looking back, I realize now that our rows were caused by Ray's mid-life crisis.

Unfairly, we women are always blamed for being miserable during the menopause. My mum said she sailed through it without being depressed or angry. I've got a few years yet until I go through the change – I have no idea how it will affect me or if I'll be as fortunate as her. But, in our house, I know we have definitely all lived through a man-opause and it was enough to cause a rift.

For a couple of years I'd been teasing Ray that he was trying to reclaim his youth. Each time he had his hair cut into a new style or came home with trendy clothes I'd rib him about it. 'You'll be buying leather trousers next,' I'd joke. We've spent our whole relationship taking the piss out of each other so it was nothing new or unkind – but I was convinced he was trying to resist the ageing process and, what was more, that it was making him desperately unhappy. I really do believe that reaching middle age is a massive problem for lots of men and it can be painful for partners who find themselves on the end of their loved one's frustrations.

As he approached his mid-fifties Ray started to hate his age. If someone jokingly accused him of being an old fart he'd get really angry. All of a sudden it was a serious issue for him.

Worse, though, was that he saw my boys, Shane and Jake, in their prime, starting to become really successful. Horrible though it is to admit, I think he was envious. Shane never stops working: he sings all over the country and in Europe. He's just been doing shows in Paris and Turkey and he's a regular at holiday camps, just like his dad once was. Jake's band, Rixton, are really good and I'm excited for them about the future. They've been signed by Scooter Braun, who also manages Justin Bieber and the Wanted and they have an album out this year. They made an amazing film for their first single in which they acted out mad scenes from videos by the likes of Miley Cyrus and Katy Perry. It was a massive hit on the download charts and we were all thrilled for them. Ray's as proud as I am of them both but I know that, deep down, he was a bit jealous of them too. He wishes his own success had come to him in his twenties, when he was free and single and able to enjoy it. His relationship with them, which had always been strong, began to falter. The boys couldn't do anything right and they started to avoid coming home, which obviously upset me. It was hard.

Ray seemed really angry all of the time. When people he didn't like came on the telly he'd shout at them. He'd moan about friends and family and seemed constantly to be in a stinking mood. 'For someone who doesn't like getting old you're behaving just like

Alf Garnett,' I told him one day. I felt more and more like I was walking on eggshells and I hated it.

He had begun to remind me of my dad. Mum and Dad had been together for half a century but he'd made many of those years a misery for her. Despite his faults I loved him but he was a drinker and would be so nasty to Mum I'd want to shout at her to leave him. Ray wasn't a drunk, and he'd never knock me about as Dad did Mum, but the way he was grouching around, finding fault with everything and everybody, was uncomfortably familiar. It brought back some very unpleasant memories.

It wasn't as if we even had our sex life to keep us together. On *Loose Women*, I was known for openly discussing aspects of our intimate relationship. I was notoriously indiscreet but I was proud of how happy we were in the bedroom department. Ray used to say that when it came to sex I was more like a man because I was happy with a quickie and didn't always need much foreplay. Well, sometimes there isn't the time and a sprint is as satisfying as a marathon, I say! I hadn't always been so self-assured. But as I became older and more confident I had fewer hang-ups about my appearance. I wasn't so worried about appearing fat in certain positions – I didn't care how I looked so long as we were both enjoying it. And, much to Ray's embarrassment, I never seemed to stop telling the nation about it! I once shared with the audience – and the rest of the country – that Ray fancied seeing me dressed up as a sexy nurse. Oh dear! It took him a while to live that one down! Now, because we were living like a couple of lodgers in the same house, that side of our marriage had ground to a shuddering halt.

Our routine would go something like this: I'd usually be in bed by midnight because I'd need to be up at seven to get Ciara ready for her day. She and I would have breakfast together before getting into the car for the journey to her school. Ray, on the other hand, was waking up at two or three in the afternoon, going out to work in Manchester, then coming home late and not going to bed until four or five in the morning. We were the proverbial ships that passed in the night. We shared a bed for two hours and didn't even know we were lying next to each other.

Eventually the Peter Kay tour came to an end. I'd hoped that when Ray stopped working in the band everything would get back to normal. But Ray's being at home a bit more actually made things worse. He'd loved having a regular gig and he was sad it was over. He would sit on the couch messing about on his guitar while I was trying to watch the television.

'You've got a studio in the house where you could do that,' I'd hiss at him. 'I'm trying to watch *Emmerdale*!'

He'd grumble something back at me, shout at poor Shane or Jake, then start pacing about the house. He was starting to get on my nerves and I realized that if one of us didn't have some time out soon we'd end up hating one another. That or having an affair.

To be frank, he's very lucky that at the time I wasn't working so much and that I was spending a lot of time at home. I'm not being big-headed and saying I could have anyone I wanted, but if, on one of the lonely nights I was away in a London hotel, I'd met somebody who made me feel even slightly attractive I might have gone for it. I remember thinking that if I went to Tesco's and someone spoke kindly to me I was in danger of starting a full-blown affair up against the frozen peas!

Again, thoughts of my first marriage came back to haunt me. I was reminded of a time when Shane was ignoring me and I ended up having a relationship with a musician. Just like now I was being starved of affection – and it was all too easy for my head to be turned by a kind and lovely keyboard player. It was 1993 and Shane had just started doing *Grease*. I was fed up and miserable staying at home, changing nappies, being ignored by my husband, so when the offer came to do a summer season in Weymouth – and take the boys with me – I jumped at the chance.

I was back on stage, beginning to feel a little like my old self, but still I was in no doubt that I was fat and frumpy. Just watching the gorgeous dancers and other performers convinced me of that. So I was gob-smacked when the handsome guy in the band started chatting me up.

'You look absolutely beautiful tonight,' he said, smiling shyly. Wow! It was ages since anybody had told me that! A shiver of excitement flooded my body, and for the first time in years I stood up tall. I must have grown two inches! While Shane was away, doing who knew what with whom, my new man was making me feel reassured, telling me I was gorgeous and sexy and deserved better. It wasn't long before we were having a very sweet but torrid affair.

I don't think I fell in love with my musician, but I loved the fact that somebody was finding me attractive. Eventually it kind of fizzled out – neither of us was looking for a relationship and, at the end of the day, I doubt I would actually have left Shane. We parted as friends and went back to our separate lives.

For a little while my musician and I carried on telephoning each other and that was how Shane caught me out. He'd started to suspect something was going on and had secretly installed a bugging device so that he could record my telephone calls. So there I was, caught red-handed – it was a real low in our time together. Shane was devastated and it prompted us both to take stock of our marriage and make a tremendous effort for one another. For the first time in ages I was being showered with love and affection but it didn't last for long. We soon went back to the old routine of him being distracted by pretty dancers, leaving me to stew unhappily at home.

I'm not proud of what happened. Having an affair was not the right and sensible thing to do, but I know exactly why it started. Shane didn't fancy me. But my musician did. The last thing I wanted now was for Ray and me to go looking for comfort in the arms of somebody else. Ray knew about my fling and I'm sure he was equally worried that history could repeat itself if I continued to feel neglected. It's a hideous thought but I really believe that everyone needs to feel loved and wanted.

I knew I had to do something major before it was too late. If rumbling along unhappily was putting us in danger of a more serious fracture, maybe it was time for drastic measures. One day, after a series of dreadful rows and after he'd spent practically no time with me for weeks on end, the two of us were alone in the house and I sat him down at the kitchen table and told him I wanted him to go.

The look on his face said it all. He couldn't believe what he'd heard. 'Christ, Coleen, you don't mean that, do you?' he said, deep pain etched on his face. 'I can't bear to go away again. We can't throw away everything we've built up together. Think of Ciara, think of the boys. We must be able to work it out.'

'I'm sorry, Ray, but what about thinking of me?' I said. He just looked at me like I'd stabbed him in the heart. He was clearly devastated, but why hadn't he shown how much he cared before? I so wanted to weaken right there and then but I knew I had to carry on – he was finally showing some sort of reaction and seemed to recognize how bad things had got. It was one of the hardest things I have ever done, though, and my heart felt like it was splitting open, especially when he mentioned the kids. But I just knew that if I didn't force him to see what he had by asking him to leave, then the marriage was certain to finally crumble. I'd already been through one divorce and I couldn't bear the idea of going through another. Leaving was the last thing I really wanted him to do but I was hoping and praying it would make him sit up and understand precisely what was happening to us. We couldn't carry on with our heads in the sand. This was either going to save us or put us out of the misery we were locked in.

'I'm sorry, Ray, but I don't feel I have a choice,' I said. The tears were streaming down my face.

'OK, Col, well if that's really what you want,' he said sadly. He looked like a broken man. It was almost as if the fight had been kicked out of him and he couldn't find any more words with which to argue.

I had missed him so much, which seems an odd thing to say when we were living together, but I'd hardly seen him lately, and when we were together, he felt like a stranger. I ached for his touch or a loving word. He was in my bed but he wasn't in my life, and he'd pushed me so far away I felt he'd already left me before I asked him to go.

I heard afterwards that Ray was an emotional wreck. He couldn't sleep or eat, which is rare for Ray. All the emotions that had seemed buried deep within him began to come to the surface. My phone buzzed with texts from him, promising that this time he would sit down with me and talk through our problems properly. I was tempted for sure. I desperately wanted to text back and say, 'Yes, all is forgiven,' but I knew I couldn't. We needed time. We weren't ready to sort things out just yet.

While all this was going on I was worried for Ciara. She's a real Daddy's girl and loves Ray very much. It was dreadful to think of her as being part of a broken home.

And I'd been there before with her brothers when they were little. When I'd first told the two boys that I was leaving their dad it caused them a lot of pain.

I can still remember them sitting on my bed as I gathered up the strength to tell them, knowing I was about to shatter their happy little world. 'Me and Daddy are not going to live together, but we both really love you,' I said, as gently as I could. Shane Junior, who was seven at the time, had curled up into a foetal position and let out a dreadful, high-pitched cry, like that of a wounded animal. Jake, who was only four and too young to know what was happening, started crying because he saw his big brother so upset. I'll never, ever forget it. I'd sworn to myself then that I would never hurt any of my children again.

With these memories still fresh in my mind, I climbed the stairs to find Shane. He was in his bedroom listening to music and I sat down next to him on the bed. 'Can you remember how you felt when I split up from your dad?' I asked him. He looked at me, at first puzzled. Then I saw a flash of understanding. I could tell he knew instinctively why I'd asked the question. He's not daft, that boy.

'You know, Mum, it affected us for about a day before we realized that nothing had changed,' he said, reaching for his iPod so that he could turn down the volume. 'The only difference was that suddenly we got two lots of Christmas presents and had bedrooms at two houses! Ciara will be fine because she's got me and Jake, so don't stay with someone for our sake.'

I knew he was right. Ciara would be heartbroken at first but in time she would be fine. Children are resilient – and apparently quite mercenary! But was that what I really wanted? Did I want to split up a second family without putting up one hell of a fight?

As an agony aunt, I'd never advise any warring couple to stay together for the sake of the kids. It rarely works and, as my own boys had shown me, children are tougher than we think. So, if we were going to stay together it had to be for reasons other than Ciara. I spent hours walking the dogs, staring out of the kitchen window as I washed the dishes, drinking endless cups of tea and smoking too many cigarettes, trying to work out the next step for Ray and me. Deep down I knew there was life in my marriage yet. I wasn't quite ready to give up on it.

After two miserable days I couldn't stand it any longer. *I miss you*, I texted. *I'm ready to talk.*

Ray's answer came through almost immediately: *I'm on my way.*

We sat in the living room and I laid everything on the table. 'I need more emotional support,' I told him. 'You've got to understand that I'm insecure because of what happened with Shane.'

This time round, instead of blowing up, Ray just reached over and took my hand.

I pushed on. 'And I'm bloody miserable about your relationship with the boys. They can't do right by you.'

He squeezed my hand and lowered his head. 'It's like living with an old moaner. I want the old Ray back. I want some sex!'

Ray wasn't going to let me have it all my way. Quite rightly he gave me both barrels. 'You've got to stop making me feel judged, then, Col. If you want me to do things like arrange weekends away or even just to take Ciara to school then bloody tell me!'

At last, we seemed to be getting somewhere. 'I think you're right about the mid-life crisis,' Ray said. 'But you're no saint, you know.'

I smiled, pulled my hand out of his and wrapped my arms around his neck. Finally we both realized we had put our marriage at risk and come very close to losing everything.

Despite sobbing in front of the nation when he watched me skating on *Dancing On Ice*, Ray's a shy, undemonstrative man. He's the exact opposite of Shane, in fact, which I suppose was what drew me to him in the first place. He promised to give me more of the little signs of affection that I craved, and I promised to stop bottling things up and to tell him when he was being an idiot. It was lovely to be so close again because neither of us had wanted our marriage to end.

'I've missed you, Nolan Face,' he told me.

'Shut up and put the kettle on,' I said.

What I've learned from all this is that I'm a very different person from the one who was married to Shane Richie. In many ways I'm a better wife to Ray than I was to Shane because I'm more at ease with myself. I'm older and more independent, for a start. I survived for years as a single parent and I have my own career. Ray knows I'm with him purely because I want to be – not because I need to be. It's an equal partnership and we both give as good as we get!

For the next few weeks Ray really tried hard to give me the affection that I needed. 'Give over, I'm only going to the kitchen to put the kettle on!' I'd joke, when I tried to break off from a cuddle on the sofa.

Ciara took it all in her stride and would roll her eyes as if we were too embarrassing. 'What are you two like? Get a room, will you?' she'd say.

Life now may not be perfect and it'll take time to get back to where we were, but it's better. OK, so Ray's not naturally Mr Romantic but he is Mr Reliable. And that's pretty important, actually. He's great around the house, he's an absolutely fantastic dad to Ciara, a good steady influence on the boys, and he sorts things out for me when everything else is in chaos. He's my anchor and my calm, and that's so precious when you do a crazy job like mine. I honestly don't know what I would do without him.

Every now and then he'll do something that drives me mad and then a little voice in my head will criticize him and remind me of my insecurities. But, in my heart, I know I'll always love him. I'd rather work very hard and fight like a tiger to make this marriage a success than give up easily. If we do split up, at least I can say we tried, which is much better than saying, 'Get over it, Ciara, and pack your bags. We're off!'

What else have I learned from all this? That there isn't a marriage on this planet in which you can afford to rest on your laurels and assume everything will be happy ever after. It's just like learning the piano: you really do have to keep working at it every single day.

So what would I say if somebody wrote to me and said her husband was going through a mid-life crisis? I'd say, 'You need to take it seriously. Your husband has not suddenly had a complete personality transplant, he's going through an experience much like any other illness. I truly believe that men suffer this kind of thing more often than women do – and I think a man's mid-life crisis can last much longer and feel much tougher. I read recently that the fastest-rising divorce rate was that of the over-sixties, the "silver separators", I think they call them. That's not at all surprising to me. I reckon that's down to mid-life wobbles for men and the fact that women are no longer willing to put up with being neglected.'

I'm glad Ray and I managed to talk about what was happening before things got out of hand and one of us looked outside the marriage for comfort. Because, as I was painfully aware, when that happens and you've betrayed each other's trust, there really isn't anywhere else to go. Now we're both trying hard to make things work – especially Ray, bless him. These days I get so many texts from him I have to tell him I'm busy!

Besides, we couldn't know it at the time but there was another problem lurking just around the corner that was to put our marriage difficulties into perspective. And it was a problem that would shake up the entire family and make me hold on for dear life to everything that was precious.

# Chapter Four

Life at home was finally beginning to get back to normal when a real bombshell landed in my lap. A few weeks after Ray had come home I was in the kitchen cooking tea when my mobile rang.

'Oh, hi, Col, it's me,' my sister Bernie said.

'Hiya, Bernie,' I replied, noting her voice sounded a bit too chirpy. We usually kept in touch by text and saved phone calls for bigger pieces of news. What's happened now? I wondered.

'Where are you?' she asked, which I thought was an odd way to start the conversation.

'Er, I'm just at home cooking dinner.'

'Are you on your own?' she went on.

'Ray and the kids are here. Why?' I now know she was checking I wasn't alone in a hotel room in London before breaking her news to me.

'Right, I've got something to tell you and it's not great,' she warned. 'I've got breast cancer.'

I stopped what I was doing and leaned against the worktop to steady myself. I felt totally devastated, but I held it together on the phone because I didn't want to upset Bernie. She told me everything – what stage the cancer was at, what treatment she needed – and reassured me that the prognosis was good.

'They tell me I have three very small tumours and that it's quite an aggressive form of breast cancer called HER2 positive. It's not great but they're going to give me chemo straight away for six months to stop it spreading and then I'll have a mastectomy and reconstruction later on,' she said.

I listened to her in a kind of trance. 'Oh, my God, Bernie. I'm so sorry,' I managed to get out.

'Don't be sorry. I don't want anyone to be down, do you hear? I don't want any of that negative stuff,' she said sternly. 'I'm going to bloody fight it, Col. I can beat this bastard thing.'

'OK, OK,' I said. 'But let me know if there's anything I can do. You only have to say and I'll be there.'

I put the phone down and walked into the living room where Ray and the boys were watching telly. When I told them I just broke down. They all stood up and gave me a hug.

I read in Bernie's book, *Now and Forever*, that she had asked one of the others to tell me she had cancer. The way she remembered it, Maureen, Linda or Brian had called me to break the news and I hadn't called her back for several days because I was so devastated. She was right that I was devastated – it hit me very hard indeed – but wrong on the other counts. I can only imagine that so much happened to her after the diagnosis that she had her facts muddled. For me, I can remember that first sickening call from Bernie as if it was yesterday.

The news gave me such a jolt that I found it difficult

86

I love this photo of Bernie and me. I miss her every moment of every day.

Hazlewood Castle, 2007. After a two-year engagement, Ray and I finally get married!

The happiest day of my life.

My son Jake's best man speech! Suffice to say he had some embarrassing stories that can't be repeated here . . .

The Nolans in the mood for dancing! Me with three of my sisters (*from left*): Linda, Bernie and Maureen.

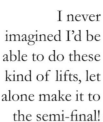

I never imagined I'd be able to do these kind of lifts, let alone make it to the semi-final!

My wonderful *Dancing On Ice* partner, Stuart Widdall. I couldn't have coped without him.

Me at my slimmest shortly after *Dancing On Ice* in 2009.

As well as lots of bumps and bruises, I also picked up a broken wrist during training but I skated on!

The Nolans back in business. *From left*: Linda, me, Bernie, Maureen.

Rocking out before the tour!

The Nolans, 1974!
*Back row, left to right*: Linda, Anne, Maureen. *Front row, left to right*: Denise, me (aged nine!) and Bernie.

Headlining the Hammersmith Apollo. I still find it so exciting to see our name up in lights.

Maureen and I with the lovely Chris Tarrant.

Me with my wonderful husband
and daughter.

My daughter Ciara on her first day
of secondary school.

Ray and I on a night out.
Love a cocktail!

My three gorgeous boys: Shane,
Ray and Jake.

Jake and Ciara will kill me for this but it's one of my favourites!

Ray got this tattoo of Ciara a few years ago. What a devoted dad!

Ray, 'Jack Nicholson' and Ciara.

Me with 'George Clooney' – a dream come true!

Ray and I with Donny Osmond, who still makes me swoon!

On the set of *This Morning* with Keith Lemon – that man is hilarious.

I was so excited to meet Barry Manilow on the set of *This Morning*!

to do anything or see anyone. We were supposed to be going to see the tour of *Dancing On Ice* the next night but I cancelled. 'I just can't face it, Ray. Let's not go,' I said.

I couldn't believe how shockingly unlucky my family had been. In 2000 Anne had noticed lumps in her breasts and had been diagnosed with cancer. She went on to have fourteen tumours removed and was put through extensive chemotherapy and radiotherapy. Then, in 2006, Linda had been diagnosed with the same hateful disease. She had another aggressive form and needed a mastectomy, chemo and radiotherapy. I'd been really upset when Anne and Linda told me they had breast cancer but with Bernie it was even more distressing.

Anne and Linda had both told me they had found a lump. I'd been waiting for news and, though it was bad, I was prepared a little. Plus, for some reason, I never had any doubt that they would both pull through. They had their treatment, soldiered on and bounced back. I hated them being ill, but I knew they would be OK.

With Bernie it felt different. Up until that horrible phone call I'd had no idea there was anything wrong with her. And it seemed too cruel that feisty, healthy Bernie faced going through the same thing. She'd always been the gobby one – as sharp as a razor and as bubbly as a glass of champagne. The thought that cancer had managed to touch her was shocking.

Bernie was now the third Nolan sister to be struck

by the disease. It made me angry to think about it. It was so unfair.

Still, I thought, on the other hand we'd been incredibly fortunate. To everybody's relief, both Anne and Linda had come through their ordeal and survived. They seemed to be healthier than ever now. Maybe we'd be lucky a third time. I hoped and prayed with everything I had that this would be the case.

Selfishly, I also started to wonder what it meant for me. I'd had my own breast-cancer scare the previous year when I'd been doing *Dancing On Ice* and it had terrified me. I was lying in the bath trying to ease my aching muscles when I felt a lump the size of a fifty-pence piece in my right breast. I'd asked Ray to feel it too and he made me promise to go to the doctor to have it checked out. I said I would but he rightly suspected I would put it off. In fact, he made the appointment for me himself and told me I was going! I'd thought the doctor would tell me I was being silly but, worryingly, he took it really seriously.

'There's definitely a mass,' he'd told me. 'I'm going to refer you to a consultant.'

Unfortunately it was going to take six weeks for a hospital appointment so we made the decision to go private instead – but even then there was a two-week wait! Those two weeks were the longest of my life. When I finally got to see my consultant at the Alexandra Hospital in Cheadle – who happened to be the doctor Linda was under at the time – I was racked with fear. I had a biopsy followed by a mammogram and an ultrasound scan. And then I waited.

The next day the consultant's secretary called. 'Coleen, I'm pleased to tell you that the mass is just dense breast tissue along with an infected gland that has swollen,' she said, as quickly as she could, keen to put me out of my misery.

'Oh, thank Christ for that!' Relief flooded me. 'Thank you so much for letting me know.'

I couldn't phone Ray fast enough. 'It's OK, it's OK,' I told him. I could almost feel his joy down the line.

Twelve months on all those fears now came rushing back. If three of my sisters had had breast cancer, the chances of me getting it too were pretty high. As a mum of three, I was shaken by that prospect and worried for the next generation. With so many Nolan women falling prey to the disease, what lay ahead for Ciara and Bernie's daughter, Erin, or any one of their female cousins? I pushed the thoughts from my head as best I could. Right now, my priority was Bernie.

The timing of her diagnosis seemed very cruel indeed. After the tour, Neil had got her a place on a new show. It was called *Popstar to Operastar* and featured a group of pop and rock singers learning how to sing operatically. Since leaving *The Bill* at the end of 2005 Bernie hadn't done much prime-time TV and it was a fantastic opportunity for her to get back on the telly and to show off her fabulous voice. Mum had trained as an opera singer and had always told Bernie she could be a soprano. Now here was her chance to prove it.

As the show went on and Bernie won the public vote week after week, we were all so proud of her. One week she sang in French and another in Italian – she was amazing! I think our phone bill almost trebled over that period – we were dialling her vote-line number so much! In week two of the show, I was sitting at home with Ray and Ciara watching when she sang 'Parla Piu Piano', the love theme from *The Godfather*. When Bernie perfectly nailed the last big note we all leaped into the air and whooped like crazy things. This was proper singing! I was so proud of her.

Bernie's performances on that show really did give me shivers: she was brilliant. At the final, she was up against Darius Campbell, who, a few years earlier, had been a *Pop Idol* finalist. Darius was good but he wasn't a patch on Bernie. When all the votes were counted she came a very close second with a margin of only half a percentage point. We all reckoned she'd been well and truly robbed!

But what she hadn't told the rest of the family was that halfway through the series she'd noticed that the skin on her left breast looked different from that on the right. People always associate breast cancer with a lump but Bernie hadn't felt anything. There was just a kind of puckering on one side, so she'd put it to the back of her mind and got on with the show. Once it was over she'd gone to the doctor who had arranged for her to have a breast scan.

It seems astonishing now to think that all through the Nolans tour, when Bernie was so radiant and belting out 'I'm In The Mood For Dancing', and throughout the *Popstar to Operastar* series, when she reduced us all to tears with her amazing performances, she already had cancer. The nasty seed of what was to become such a terrible part of our family history had already been sown.

But it was no time to be gloomy – Bernie wouldn't let us. Despite the diagnosis she carried on being the life and soul of the party, filling her time with work, family and friends. She was amazing and so positive that the rest of us had no choice but to be positive, too. Out of all of us girls, she had always been the one who was so healthy and bursting with the joys of life. If there was a party to be had, then Bernie would be at the centre of it. If there was a table to stand on and belt out a song, it was Bernie who'd be first up. She was always first on the dance floor and the last woman standing at any celebration. We all agreed that this time cancer had chosen the wrong woman to mess around with!

Obviously, when I was alone at home, there were times when I suddenly remembered what was going on and I would feel afraid and upset for her. The unease would hit me right in the middle of my stomach and make me feel sick for a while but I tried not to let the rest of the family see how much I was affected. Bernie wasn't letting it ruin her life so we had to get on with ours, too. It was up to all of us to take our lead from her.

Bernie being Bernie, she wanted to take the fight to the cancer. She wasn't going to take it lying down. Once she and Steve had broken the news to Erin and to the rest of the family, she did a very frank interview with the newspapers. Word had started to get out and she wanted to take control of the situation. It was also important to her to try to send a positive message that might help other women who were going through the same thing.

The following Sunday she was splashed all over the front page of the *News of the World*. It was horrible seeing the words 'BERNIE: MY BREAST CANCER BATTLE' printed so large for all the world to see. But it was what she wanted and she didn't hold back from revealing exactly how she felt about the situation. 'Cancer's a scary word but it can bugger off!' she said. 'I don't care – just get this shit out of me.'

The response she got from the public was overwhelming. Long-time fans were sad to hear she was ill but others, many of whom were facing the same battle, wrote to thank her for being so optimistic and strong. Heartened by the reaction, Bernie went on to do several television interviews. 'I'm going to kick this cancer's arse,' she said in one. She was determined there was only going to be one winner in that fight, and it wasn't going to be the Big C.

The chemo treatment appeared to be working. There had been a slight disappointment for Bernie after she discovered she was allergic to one of the drugs that was being trialled. Her attitude was to take anything the doctors could give her to help her win her fight. However, the medical staff assured her they still had plenty of ammunition in their arsenal. In the end she had a cocktail of Herceptin, Carboplatin and Taxol and, after just two weeks of treatment, the scans showed that the tumours had shrunk by more than three centimetres. Everyone was surprised and delighted.

'See, what did I tell you?' Bernie would say. 'Positive thoughts, positive thoughts!'

But as much as they were saving her life, the harsh chemicals were also making her lose her hair. For the first few chemo sessions Bernie had worn a cold cap to try to stop it falling out. But the treatment had made the sessions longer and more uncomfortable and she'd quickly abandoned it. Despite knowing it was likely to happen, it was still a shock for her when her blonde locks began to disappear.

'God, Bernie, you've always had such fabulous hair,' I said to her, when she called to tell me. 'But you just wait, it'll all come back again even more gorgeous than before.'

It was the first time I saw her spirits take a bit of a dip. A woman's hair is so important to her that losing it must feel like losing part of your femininity. Plus it was constant evidence of her illness. Every time she saw a bald patch it was another reminder of the cancer. In the end she tried to grab the initiative by asking Steve to shave her hair off completely. When it was done she sent me a picture on my phone. She actually had quite a beautifully shaped head, but I know it upset her to see how cancer was wrestling for control of her.

For a while, she wore a blonde wig. Erin was completely cool about seeing her mum in a bandanna at home but uneasy about Bernie going out bald in public, which was understandable. Her hairdresser found an amazing synthetic wig that exactly matched Bernie's previous shade and style, and it reinvigorated her, making her feel like the old Bernie once again.

There was another big Nolan event coming up and Bernie was keen to look her best. Maureen was about to be married to her long-time love Ritchie. They'd been together ever since meeting in Blackpool during a Nolans' summer season. That was more than twenty years ago and, despite having their son Danny, they'd never found a reason to get married. Suddenly, on Maureen's fifty-fifth birthday Ritchie had popped the question. They planned to get married in Spain, where they have an apartment, and we were all sick with excitement!

Bernie chose Maureen's hen party to try out her new wig. It was so realistic she almost had to take it off to prove it wasn't her own hair! 'Looking great, Bernie,' said Ritchie, when she arrived for the do. 'Why did you think you needed a wig?'

'This is a wig!' she said, delighted.

'Fuck off!' said Ritchie. 'I can't believe that, it's fantastic!'

Bernie had been fretting that she wouldn't be allowed to travel to Spain but in the end the doctors gave her their blessing and she was able to go.

It was just as well because Maureen had asked

Bernie, Linda and me to be bridesmaids and it wouldn't have been the same without her there. Ciara and Erin were to be flower girls, and Maureen's son Danny was going to give her away. It was shaping up to be a wonderful family celebration.

Once we all got out there Bernie kept stressing about how she'd look in the photographs and whether she should wear her wig or a bandanna or simply go without either. During the day, it was so hot that she couldn't stand the synthetic wig and sat by the pool with a pretty scarf wrapped around her head. She looked lovely.

'I don't know why you're worrying,' I told her. 'Just walk up the aisle like that.'

By the time the wedding day arrived she'd made her decision. She'd wear her wig made of real hair, which had been styled to look like how she'd had it on tour – smooth and blonde and shiny. Our bridesmaids' dresses were really pretty and, as Bernie followed Maureen down the aisle, looking stunning in her lavender gown, no one would have known she was ill.

In September it was the *TV Choice* awards at London's Dorchester Hotel and Bernie and I were both going. *Loose Women* had been nominated for Best Daytime Show. I'd chosen a full-length black evening dress and had my hair and makeup done specially. As I looked in the mirror at the stylist putting the finishing touches to my hair my heart went out to Bernie. It must be so difficult on occasions like this when you really wanted to look your best.

I was travelling with Denise Welch, who was up for an award for her drama *Waterloo Road*, and we'd arranged to see Bernie at the do. Suddenly I saw her, striding down the red carpet, looking absolutely amazing. She had on a designer frock – long and black with sparkly shoulders and sleeves – and her makeup was exquisite. But all eyes were on her because she'd turned up without her wig and was absolutely bald. I almost wept at her bravery – and her beauty.

'Bernie, you look stunning!' I said, as we gave each other a hug. Reporters were clamouring to interview her and she was soon whisked away from me. I proudly watched her beaming into the cameras and explaining her decision to ditch the wig.

'I've spent the past few weeks saying I'm happy with no hair, so I felt it was important to come here and show I meant it,' she said. 'You know what? After ten minutes no one notices about the hair.'

Bernie was adamant she wanted to send other women in her situation a strong message – that she was in control and not frightened of showing the effects of chemo. Chemo, as she had told us countless times, was her best friend and was going to save her life.

'Before chemo I used to worry about what I looked like and what people thought but I don't really care any more. This is who I am,' she said. 'I wanted to say to all those women in the same situation as me, be who you are. You do what you want to do – sod what people think. If you want to go bald then just do it. Be yourself and hang the rest of them!'

It was a magical, unforgettable night all round. Denise won for Best Actress and then, to our delight, *Loose Women* also scooped the Best Daytime Show award. It was one of those evenings when anything seemed possible – and, awards aside, that was down to Bernie's courage.

The following week she had her last chemo session. Despite her defiant positivity, the treatment had been tough. After the second round of chemo she started getting mouth ulcers, which was a side effect of the drugs. They made eating and drinking very difficult for her and for a while she had to take a break, which made her furious and very frustrated. All of us felt desperate for her but Bernie, determined as ever, wasn't having any of it.

'So what if I'm bald and I've got mouth ulcers,' she'd tell us. 'Give me that chemo – it's going to keep me alive!'

She was convinced that being a cup-half-full type of person was the only way she was going to pull through. She had her family, her husband, her career, and she'd be damned if she'd admit defeat.

Bernie completed her course of chemo and around this time was tested and found out that her type of breast cancer wasn't genetic. 'Oh, thank God for that.' I breathed a sigh of relief when she told me. It was such a blessing and means that the next generation – Ciara, Erin and their female cousins – are no more at risk of developing the disease than anyone else.

Not that any of us can afford to be complacent. The geneticist said there may be a rogue gene from my father's side of the family, which hadn't been detected yet. So while I may not be a carrier of the BRCA mutation I make sure I have check-ups every six months. It's the one appointment I will not cancel for anything or anybody. Even if I was interviewing the prime minister at Number 10 I'd not miss my mammogram. I check myself all the time and I know our family's history makes me a priority in the eyes of the doctors. And if there's anything I'm worried about in between those six months I'm right down there at the doctor's to have it checked out. It's a message I've drummed into Ciara and I know, when the time comes, she'll be super aware of the dangers.

One night I was lying in bed with Ray when I suddenly felt a new wave of fear crashing over me. 'Do you think I should have a preventative double mastectomy just in case?' I asked him. 'I'm not brave like Bernie. I couldn't bear the thought of going through what she's going through and I want to be here for you and the kids.'

Ray didn't answer for a few minutes. I could tell he was thinking carefully about what I'd said. 'You know, I reckon only you can answer that, Col,' he said. 'You need to talk to the doctors and get the best possible advice, but I'm here for you whatever you decide to do. I love you, not your breasts.'

'Right, I'm going to call them tomorrow,' I decided. 'If that's what it takes to get peace of mind and to secure our future then that's what I'm going to do.'

To me the choice was a no-brainer. If my breasts were ticking time-bombs waiting to rob me of a long and healthy life with my children and husband, they would have to go. Sharon Osbourne and Angelina Jolie have both now done it, and there's barely a day goes by that I don't read about another woman who has chosen to have the surgery.

I made an appointment with my doctor and explained my situation. 'Three out of six sisters have been diagnosed with breast cancer,' I said. 'I'm willing to do whatever – should I have both my breasts removed?'

'Well, you already know that you don't carry the gene mutation and neither do your sisters,' the doctor said. 'And, to be frank, a double mastectomy wouldn't stop cancer from attacking another part of your body. The best thing is to be vigilant and have regular scans. Check yourself and make sure you know what you're looking for.'

I'd be pretty pissed off if I had my breasts removed only to get cancer somewhere else, I thought. I decided to trust the doctors and take their advice. But I'm telling you, if there's ever any doubt about it in the future, they're off.

In October, having finished her chemo treatments, Bernie faced surgery. She kept saying to us, 'By Christmas it will all be over!' We prayed for her that it would be. She went back into hospital to have a mastectomy and reconstruction and her surgeon also removed thirteen lymph nodes, which, thank God, turned out to be healthy. She'd been told if the cancer had spread they would have to take her nipple as well. She felt that was an important part of the reconstruction and worried about what a new boob would look like without one. When she awoke she discovered the nipple still in place and she had a fantastic new breast.

We were all so relieved for her. In eight months Bernie had gone from horrific diagnosis to being cancer-free. The scans showed her body was clear of the disease – they'd got every bit of the damn thing.

The Nolan jungle drums sounded and the brilliant news spread quickly. Linda rang me. 'Hi, Col, it's me,' she said. 'Have you heard yet about Bernie? It's fantastic. They've got it all.'

Then Maureen would be texting me. *Can breathe again!* she wrote. *She's going to be OK.*

I so wanted it to be true. I caught the wave of optimism and texted Bernie. *Congratulations*, I wrote. *Let's have a party!* But Bernie, usually the party girl, was just calmly happy. If you asked her if she was cured or if doctors had given her the all-clear, she'd say, 'No, I'm in remission.' It was enough, for now.

Bernie's illness, and the way she had coped with it, put everything into perspective for me that year and made me value my own family even more. When things like that happen you just want to grab hold of your loved ones and never let them out of your sight. Once the news had gone public the *Loose Women* girls, my other little family, had been the first to tell me how sorry they were. Often it was difficult to spend much time with them, away from my own brood, but everyone at work was so supportive, which I really appreciated.

'How's Bernie doing?' the makeup girls or the floor manager would ask, as soon as I was in the building. 'Send her our love.' It was kind of them but, all the same, I was beginning to wonder how happy I was travelling up and down the country each week leaving Ray, Ciara and the boys at home.

My brave sister had made me realize that life was too short to be away from the one place that makes you the happiest. I began to think long and hard about my job at *Loose Women*.

For a decade I'd loved it. It was a show full of fun and joy, and that hour on screen still felt so good because of the chemistry between all of us girls on the panel. We knew what our jobs were. I was the common, funny one. Carol McGiffin was the grumpy ladette and Sherrie Hewson was a bit eccentric, but just fabulous. Over the years there had been many different bums on those seats. Denise Welch, Jane McDonald, Lynda Bellingham and Andrea McLean were great mates. My favourite was our original anchor, Kaye Adams. She was so clever, an absolute genius who taught me so much about presenting when we first worked together in the early days. I found it difficult when she left to have a baby in 2006 and missed working alongside her.

I'd had so many fantastic years on the show. It was the biggest – and longest – job I'd ever had and it had turned me once more into a household name. I loved having complete strangers coming up to me in the street urging me to tell Carol where to shove it or to help Denise sort her life out. The fans also felt they knew Ray, because I'd spent so many years talking about him. He'd get mobbed wherever he went!

Working on *Loose Women* is a bit like being part of the Nolans. It's a big, welcoming family that puts its arms around you, gives you a hug and makes you feel secure. The people on the programme are just fabulous, from the runners to the canteen staff to the cameramen. You couldn't ask to work for a nicer bunch. The editors and producers, too, are clever and supportive. But, just like in the Nolans, there are always going to be squabbles. When you get a gaggle of opinionated women together it's inevitable. It wasn't the bitch-fest that some newspapers described it as but there were rows. There would be times when we'd fall out for real over something that we'd been discussing on screen, or the constant sarky comments would go a step too far and someone would storm into their dressing room. But, really, we loved one another.

Looking back I was obviously feeling vulnerable because of my worries about Bernie, but any bickering instantly made me feel like walking out of the door and getting the first train straight back home to Cheshire.

The biggest reason I left *Loose Women* was to focus on my family. Leaving was a massive financial consideration, though. For a decade it had given me a steady wage and I couldn't afford to throw it all away without thinking things over very carefully. People tend to think you earn a fortune on the telly, and they're partly right – TV work pays very well in comparison to, say, nursing or teaching. But there is always the mortgage to be paid and, as the main breadwinner, I had responsibilities. Thankfully, for the past two years I'd been working my socks off. And *Dancing On Ice* and the Nolans' tour had given me enough money to think about taking some time off.

Ciara was about to begin her first year at high school and I felt she needed her mum around more than ever. For years I'd written a parenting column for the *Mirror* and I'd sometimes feel a twinge of guilt about my own skills in that department. I'm not the first working mum to feel that way, and I think women are usually too hard on themselves, but I needed to devote more time to being a mum. I wanted to be at home to help her through the transition to big school and, after all the hard work, I was in the lucky position of being able to do just that.

So, I had a massive decision to make. Yes, *Loose Women* was a fantastically popular show and, yes, it was regular work, but Bernie's brush with disaster had been a wake-up call. I quickly picked up the phone before I had time to change my mind. 'Neil,' I said to my agent. 'I want to leave the show NOW.'

# Chapter Five

Television is a fickle boss. It's nice to think you're the one in control of your career but the reality is you can be flavour of the month one minute and the voiceover to a catfood ad the next – if you're lucky! I've come to realize that it's just business – but in the early days any backwards step was a terrible blow to my confidence.

The last time my name was mentioned in the same breath as *This Morning*, ITV's flagship daytime programme, had been to receive terrible criticism. 'COLEEN AXED FROM *THIS MORNING*', the newspaper headlines had screamed. My God, I wanted an enormous hole to open up and swallow me. Being sacked so publicly was humiliating and, at the time, I really believed it spelled the end of my fledgling television career.

It had all started so well. Back in 2001 I'd somehow landed one of the best jobs in TV – co-hosting *This Morning* alongside sixties icon Twiggy. After thirteen years the legendary Richard and Judy had left the show to go to Channel 4, and every TV presenter in Britain seemed to be fighting for the job. One day the controller of ITV daytime, Maureen Duffy, a lovely, elegant woman, who turned out to be really kind to me, called me in for a chat.

'Have you heard that Richard and Judy are leaving?' she asked.

I wondered what that had to do with me, and said something like, 'Yes, it's such a shock. They'll be hard boots to fill.'

'Well, how would you feel about giving it a go?' she said. Apparently they were looking for somebody who was homely and fun. I'll give 'em homely if that's what they want, I remember thinking. In fact, I'd stand on my head and sing the national anthem if it came to it! It was such an incredible break and I could hardly believe my luck. The new job would mean we had to move, lock, stock and barrel, to London but when a chance like that comes knocking you don't say no.

'Thank you,' I said, as coolly as I could. Inside my head fireworks and klaxons were going off but I was determined to remain calm. 'I'd love to have a go.'

Of course, I had to go through the usual screen tests to prove I was up to the job. Luckily, the test involved pretending to interview the editor of the programme, Johnny McCune, and we clicked straight away. We did a few other segments together and I loved it. Johnny seemed pleased, too, and told me I'd hear soon about the job.

I travelled home to Blackpool in a state of excitement. It seemed unreal that I would be given such a plum job ahead of so many others. I couldn't wait to hear if it was actually going to happen. I didn't have to wait for long. The next day Maureen's assistant phoned to offer me the role. I would start that September, in about eight weeks' time.

It meant, however, that Ray, eight-week-old Ciara, the boys and I needed a home down south – and fast! I look back now and can't quite believe what happened next but, in a fact-is-stranger-than-fiction kind of way, we ended up moving into my old marital home with my ex-husband Shane and his girlfriend Claire. It just seemed to make perfect sense. Finding a place for a family of five to rent quickly would have cost a fortune and it meant the boys could spend more time with their dad.

I can remember pulling up outside the house where I'd lived with Shane for so long and feeling sick with nerves. I'd had happy times and sad times in that house and it was just so weird to go back there with Ray and my new baby. The funniest point was when Claire, who was only trying to be kind, bless her, offered to show me where the guest room was.

'It's OK,' I said, smiling grimly. 'I think I know where to find it.'

Claire was really sweet over the next few days and we ran around like crazy, trying to get the boys ready for their new schools. I'm not sure how I would have managed without her. She even went shopping with me for new uniforms while Ray stayed at home to take care of Ciara. Ray, too, was an absolute angel. There can't be too many men who would agree to move in with their wife's ex-husband and happily hold the baby while she got to have a shiny new exciting career.

It was probably just as well that things were so chaotic: rushing around to get the family settled was a great distraction from my nerves. When I stood still longer than a moment or two I was filled with absolute terror! How would I cope with a two-hour live show? Would the, admittedly odd, combination of Twiggy and me work on screen? What the bloody hell was I doing taking on such a thing? The questions were endless and, lying in the spare room in my ex-husband's house, they kept me awake at night.

I was given loads of training – presenting workshops, filming pilots and one-to-one coaching – but I didn't get to meet Twiggy until a few days before we went on air. When we did get together she was calm while I was shaking like a jelly! I wondered again about the wisdom of using two such very different women as anchors. She was fifty-one, I was thirty-five. She was cool, tall and very media savvy. I was a lot more down to earth. Stop panicking, the producers must know what they're doing, I told myself.

It was only the day before the live show that we got to sit on the sofa together. Things didn't go well. Twiggy was quite short-sighted and when the autocue was right for her, it made reading very difficult for me. She needed the print to be so large that I could only read about two words at a time! Plus, she didn't seem able to get the timing right for the ad breaks so that was left to me. This is going to be a nightmare, I thought.

After only one show the critics savaged us. They said Twiggy and I just didn't gel. Really? Well, I could have told them that for nothing. They rightly criticized my inexperience but saved most of their bile for poor Twiggy, who, they said, was wooden. The show's website was inundated with complaints from viewers. 'Sorry, Twiggy, I'm sure you're very nice, just not on live television over two hours,' said one. 'And let's face it, you don't look like you're enjoying it either.'

Richard and Judy's final show had pulled in something like 1.8 million viewers. With Twiggy and me at the helm, viewing figures for *This Morning* had dipped below the one million mark. The producers continued to reassure me but I wasn't blind. I could see that something would have to give.

Sure enough, within four weeks of starting, poor Twiggy was gone and they replaced her with the former *Blue Peter* presenter John Leslie. It was a relief to work with someone who'd done so much live telly. John later found himself up to his neck in indecent-assault allegations – which were never proven – but to me he was always the perfect gent.

I loved everything about that show. The crew, the ladies in the phone room, the hair and makeup girls – they were all so welcoming and made me feel part of the team from day one. With John by my side, I felt that things were going really well. We seemed to really gel and there was a spark between us that had been missing with Twiggy. The boys loved their new school and I felt secure enough to start looking for a house to buy so that we would have a home of our own. Embarrassingly, Shane and Claire would often bicker and it had started to feel claustrophobic with so many people living on top of one another.

Fate appeared to be shining on us because, just at that moment a man called Pete Suddaby, who had once gone out with my sister Maureen, decided he wanted to sell his gorgeous mock-Tudor detached house in Ickenham, Middlesex, just five minutes' away from where we were living in Shane's house. Not long after we moved out, Claire packed her bags and left, too. I couldn't blame her. After five years she was finally fed up with Shane messing her around.

I felt more confident about the future than I had done in years but as is often the way in television, just when you think you can relax the rug gets pulled from under you. One day I came into the studio and I was called upstairs and told that Fern Britton was coming back. I was thanked for my time on the show, but told that I wouldn't be continuing in the same role. I was out of the building within the hour and home being hugged by Ray an hour after that. But that's showbiz – you never really know what's going to happen and it's rarely personal. Things change and people come and go. I'd been tarred by the Twiggy backlash so it wasn't really a surprise. I just hoped it didn't mean I was finished for ever.

The end of *This Morning* signalled a real bleak patch in our lives because Ray and I were forced to sell our lovely new home in Ickenham and move the kids back up to Blackpool. I felt embarrassed, like I'd failed and gone home with my tail between my legs. Once I was back at home though family life soon put it into perspective. Life goes on – the school run needs doing and socks need washing. The life of a mum is one I'll never tire of so back to fishfingers it was!

Fortunately, we'd never sold the house in Blackpool because Ray had wanted us to have a northern bolthole from which he could keep an eye on his mum, Irene. The kids settled in again brilliantly but, for about a year, we struggled to get by. Neither of us was working and there were very few fresh TV offers. I was given one or two slots on local telly, which paid around £100, but that was it. Ray had a few gigs but we were basically living hand to mouth. Thank God we'd finished paying off the mortgage on the Blackpool house but there was no money for treats or little luxuries. Things eventually improved and later on there would be other TV jobs, including *Loose Women*, but it was a real blow to my confidence.

So fast forward to 2010 and by now I'd licked my wounds and had my share of successful TV work. I'd gone from an inexperienced rookie shaking in my boots to being quite the old hand in front of a camera. Nevertheless, when Neil phoned, almost nine years later to the day, to tell me that the producers of *This Morning* wanted me back, it came as a massive shock.

'They want to introduce a section where viewers call and email to talk about featured items and sofa guests,' he said. 'It'll be called the Hub and they want you to host it on Monday and Tuesday.'

Over the silence down the telephone line, he could obviously sense my uneasiness. He knew I'd been so burnt by the bad press around Twiggy and I presenting *This Morning*, and he knew I never imagined in a million years that they'd want me back, or that I'd want to put myself in the line of fire. Back then I'd had a different agent but he still knew what a nightmare it had been for me.

'You must be joking,' I said, shivering at the mere suggestion. 'Why on earth would I put myself in the firing line all over again?' I couldn't believe he was even saying it! 'You are joking, aren't you?'

'No, I'm not! Listen to me – they wouldn't want you if they didn't think you were right for the show again,' he said. 'The old stuff was years ago. This time it's going to be an entirely different role and they want you back in the *This Morning* family.'

It did seem like the ideal job. By now I was more certain than ever that I wanted to leave *Loose Women*, and having a regular gig like *This Morning* to go to was the perfect safety net for me. It would give me a great exit plan and, despite the way things had ended previously, it felt a little bit like going home.

'God, yes, let's give it a go – but Twiggy won't be there, will she?' I joked.

There's something so brilliant about *This Morning*. It's the busiest show I've been on in my life but everybody just goes in, does their bit and goes out. There are no egos, no prima donnas, no squabbles and no bitching. Honestly, it's a breath of fresh air. On that first day back I walked in and saw the same old faces: the same floor manager, same hair and makeup team, same crew members. They welcomed me like I'd just popped out to the shops to get a pint of milk!

I like to think I was asked back because I never, ever burn my bridges. After I'd left in 2001 I was offered a fortune by a Sunday newspaper to talk about my time on *This Morning.* I turned them down – I knew it would be career suicide to start gossiping about my former colleagues and bosses. Besides, that's just the way it is in this line of work. Whenever anything comes to an end I'm never angry or bitter. 'Thanks for that, it was great, time to move on,' is my mantra. Like I said, I know it isn't personal. It's only when they get in someone who's crap that you think, Well, she's obviously slept with someone to land that job!

For the next six months my life was as busy as ever. I'd be travelling down from Wilmslow to London every week to do my two days on the Hub and a few days on *Loose Women,* then getting the train home to be a weekend mum to Ciara and a wife to Ray. It was at the start of one of those weekends that a freak accident gave me a proper jolt and scared me half to death.

It happened at our local stables in Cheshire. When I was a little girl I was horse mad. I'd hang out at a stables in Blackpool and spend hours grooming the horses and mucking them out. Ciara had inherited my obsession, and one of the best things about my having a regular job was that we'd been able to buy her a pony, Paddy. God, does she love that horse! She'd spend all her time with him if she could – in fact, I think she'd even move into the stables if I let her!

One day I was at the stables with her when I noticed one of the other horses had put its head over the door and got his head collar stuck on the lock. With hindsight, what I should have done was to unfasten the collar first, but I didn't. Stupidly I put my hand through the collar while he was still wearing it to try to set him free. As I did so he freaked and pulled back into the stables, dragging me with him and smashing my hand against the door. Luckily it was quite an old bit of wood so my hand went clean through it – if it had been a bit more robust I would have lost my fingers.

By now I'd managed to free myself and I looked down at my hand to inspect the damage. Two of my fingers looked very strange indeed, sort of flattened and almost as if they were empty. Oh, God, that doesn't look right, I thought, so I pushed them back into a kind of finger shape. It was odd because it didn't hurt at the time. I suppose I must have been in shock.

I could hear two of the stable guys in the yard so I started shouting for help. 'Wayne, Wayne,' I called. 'I think I've really hurt my finger.'

Wayne came over, smiling. 'Have you really hurt it or are you just being a wuss?' he said. I showed it to him and he went white. 'Oh, Jesus, we need to get you to the hospital now!' he said.

He dashed inside and got an ice pack, which he

clamped on to my hand. By the time we got to Macclesfield Hospital my fingers hadn't simply reinflated themselves, they appeared to be about four times bigger than the others.

The nurse in A and E said I'd need an X-ray. 'You'll have to remove that ring from your finger,' she said. But my fingers were so swollen there was no way it was coming off. Then they produced a really blunt old ring cutter and that poor little nurse was trying to chop through the gold without much luck. By now I was beginning to regain the feeling in my hand and every time she touched it I nearly jumped off my chair. I don't know whose nerves were more tattered – hers or mine!

'If we can't do it we'll have to call the fire brigade,' she said, clearly distressed by now.

Wayne, who's a huge man, chipped in, 'I'll have a go if you like.'

'Shut up,' I said. 'Let her call the fire brigade!' In the end Wayne managed to cut it off and I didn't get to be rescued by a handsome fireman. Damn!

I was taken to the X-ray department and afterwards a nice doctor called my name so that he could show me the results. I could see one finger had a single fracture in it but I couldn't make out what I was seeing in the space next to it.

'That's what's left of your other one,' said the doctor. 'It's unrecognizable as a finger. I'm afraid it's just splinters of bone.'

Oh, Jesus, Mary and Joseph. That was a bit of a

shock. I thought they'd just strap me up and send me home, but I was going to need an operation to insert pins and a metal bar!

But by then it was late Friday night and the orthopaedic department had closed. 'I'm sorry,' the doctor said. 'We'll have to discharge you and call you back in when there's a surgeon available.'

That night the pain was even worse than childbirth. The gas and air they'd given me in the hospital had worn off, as had the shock, and my hand hurt like hell. The next morning I rang Neil in tears to warn him that I probably wouldn't be able to work the following week. When I told him I was waiting at home while the hospital tried to find a surgeon he was incredulous. 'Coleen, you've got private medical insurance. What the hell are you waiting for?' he said. Oh, yeah. For some reason I hadn't thought of that!

After that things moved quickly. I still hadn't heard from Macclesfield Hospital but the Alexandra Hospital in Cheadle had me in for X-rays on the Sunday, in front of a doctor on the Monday and in surgery by Tuesday for a two-and-a-half-hour operation to insert five pins and a metal bar. I was told that with crush injuries there's only a limited window of opportunity and, had I left it much longer, I might have lost my finger! I didn't know whether to laugh or cry when, ten days later, Macclesfield Hospital finally got in touch to say they had arranged an appointment for me. It was a bit bloody late!

Not being able to use my right hand was really

difficult. I'm so right-handed it's not even funny, and for three or four weeks I was helpless. I couldn't even dress myself. Bless Linda, who came to stay and helped me look after Ciara and keep everybody sane. She even sat through the night with me when the pain was too much to bear. One night the drugs they'd given me weren't touching the sides so we sat up and watched about four films on TV.

The next morning I went back to the hospital to be checked out. The surgeon took one look at my swollen hand and said, 'That bandage is too tight, we'll have to cut it off.' For some reason I went into an absolute blind panic.

It's the one and only time in my life that I've had a full-blown panic attack. Oh, my God, it was hideous. As the doctor was cutting the bandage the pain was indescribable and I began to cry. The next thing I knew I'd lost my breath and couldn't get it back. I was struggling to breathe and getting more and more panicky by the moment.

'Coleen, listen to us, you're having a panic attack!' the doctor was shouting at me. It was ridiculous. I was lying there with all this expensive equipment and oxygen tanks around me and it took a nurse to run in with a brown-paper bag.

'Blow in this, Coleen,' she said. It was like something in a comedy sketch.

Once I had my breathing under control the doctor was able to finish his examination. He said a combination of no sleep and pain had brought on the attack and told me I needed to rest. 'I'm going to give you an injection to knock you out,' he said. 'You need a proper night's sleep.'

Well, he gave me the jab and, boy, did I sleep! After all the pain and drama it was wonderful to just float off into oblivion. The whole episode seemed ridiculous. I'd gone from calling Ray when I was at the stables to say I'd broken my finger to needing almost a month off work.

It wasn't long before life returned to normal and I was back in my old routine of staying in London for a few nights a week. It sounds like a treat, and for a while it is. I don't have to think about getting everybody's tea or loading the dishwasher or tumble-dryer, but, believe me, it soon becomes quite boring. I'd end up putting my pyjamas on, ordering room service and watching the telly sitting on my bed. OK, that's not so very different from my life at home but I missed lying on the sofa with Ray and Ciara and being able to make a decent cup of tea when I wanted one.

I don't think anyone was really happy about the situation. Ciara would send me plaintive little texts complaining of tummy-ache or saying that she'd had a problem at school or at the stables. More than two hundred miles away, I wasn't in much of a position to help her but I knew what she was really saying: 'I miss you, Mum, and I wish you were here.' I longed to be with Ray and Ciara. I spent too many nights alone in London and too many weekends shattered and unable to join in with normal family life.

At least Bernie seemed to be getting better and returning to her old bouncy self. By February 2011 she was back on stage doing a tour of *Calendar Girls*. It was perfect for her. It's the true story of a group of Women's Institute ladies who shoot a saucy charity calendar. You might have seen the 2003 film, starring Helen Mirren, Julie Walters, Celia Imrie and Penelope Wilton. In the play, the women all strip off but cleverly position themselves behind pots of jam or Victoria sandwich cakes – and, for Bernie, it involved her going topless on stage!

There were some old friends on the tour with her: *Loose Women*'s Lynda Bellingham, Ruth Madoc, Lisa Riley and Jennifer Ellison, whom Bernie had worked with on *Brookside*. Bernie's character was Cora the piano player, which meant that at least she'd have her back to the audience, but it was still a massively brave thing for her to do, considering what she'd just been through. Nothing seemed to faze her, though, and she said later she found it empowering and liberating to get her kit off on stage and be like one of the others. Plus, the subject matter of the play seemed fitting: the calendar was originally made to raise money for a cancer charity following the death of one woman's husband from the disease. It's a touching story and came along for Bernie at just the right time.

She finished the *Calendar Girls* tour in April and, typical of my whirlwind sister, immediately booked a long holiday in Florida with Erin and Steve. It was as if she was cramming every minute of her life with memories for her family to share in the future. When she returned to the UK she threw a party for two hundred friends and relatives at a gorgeous hotel near her home in Weybridge. It was Bernie's belated fiftieth birthday celebration – and her fuck-off-cancer party!

She and Steve had booked a great sixteen-piece band to play and we all moved Heaven and Earth to be there. After such a tough year no one was going to miss that party. There were friends and relatives invited from Ireland, from Blackpool and all over the UK. I'd heard that Anne was definitely going and was slightly worried that things might be awkward between us. I hadn't seen much of her since before the tour and, as these things tend to do, our disagreement had festered. Still, I tried to push it from my mind. What was important now was Bernie. It was such a joyous occasion that it felt like a wedding!

Most of us gave a song that night, my brother Brian, Maureen and Linda. I'd always been the least confident singer of the girls – but even I got up on stage! Anne also did a number and reminded us all of her lovely voice. I could feel my unease fading and we spent the night politely avoiding one another. Shane Junior and Jake got up and did a song and Bernie did, too. She sang so beautifully and I was overwhelmed by how she looked and sounded after everything she'd been through. It was just great to see. By now her hair had grown back, although it was very short. It suited her, actually. Her makeup artist Sally had spent hours giving her false eyebrows and eyelashes to replace those that had been lost to the chemo. In fact her makeup was quite amazing that night: Bernie was stunning.

I remember looking at her in her favourite place, centre stage, doing what she loved most, and daring to think that she really had kicked cancer's arse. During her treatment a tiny percentage of me had begun to doubt that the Nolans would be third time lucky. Then I'd be reminded of Bernie's positivity, give myself a slap and send the negative thoughts packing.

The highlight of the night was when Bernie's Erin, accompanied by her dad Steve on keyboards, sang 'When Somebody Loved Me' from *Toy Story 2*. Bless! It was so touching. Bernie just cried and cried and cried – something you didn't often see her do. Then she picked herself up, wiped away the tears and was back on the dance floor.

'Does that woman ever stand still?' I laughed with Linda and Maureen. It seemed our sister had more energy than the rest of us put together. But it was so good to see her well again and full of optimism for the future. We couldn't get her off the dance floor until two a.m. and it was gone four when we eventually dragged ourselves to our beds. What a night!

But back at work the time had come to say goodbye to *Loose Women*. I knew I couldn't carry on for much longer. While Bernie had been so ill, it had been getting more and more difficult to carry on being the funny one on the left-hand side of the panel. Sometimes I'd be lost in my own thoughts about chemo and cancer and I'd realize I was right in the middle of some silly item that I really didn't care much about.

One day Maureen rang and asked me what was wrong. She'd been watching *Loose Women* and was worried about me. 'What's up with you?' she asked. 'You were really quiet today. It's like you're leaning back and letting everybody else on the show get on with it.' She was right. That was just what I'd been doing.

Witnessing Bernie's incredible lust for life had reminded me, again, that I needed to spend more time with my own little family. I needed to sort my priorities. I told Neil that I was finally ready to leave when the series ended in July. He was great. He understood my reasons and made the necessary arrangements for me to go.

'COLEEN CUTS LOOSE' ran the headlines, when it was eventually announced in March that I was leaving. I was quite surprised by the fuss that was made and not a little scared. Suddenly it seemed so final. I'd spent a long time agonizing about my decision but now it was out in the open it was too late to change my mind. I hope I haven't put my family on the breadline again, I thought. This business is so unpredictable that, for all I knew, I could have been killing my career.

I always say that after my horrible first experience on *This Morning*, it was *Loose Women* that saved my life. My confidence was at rock bottom and, so far as TV work went, I really believed that I was unemployable. I felt washed up and tarred by my failure at *This Morning*.

Then a miracle happened when Johnny McCune, the editor I'd got on with so brilliantly at *This Morning*, moved to become executive producer on *Loose Women*. He gave me a chance to prove myself and come back all guns blazing. The rest, as they say, is history.

The past ten years had been a crazy journey. The original *Loose Women* family had picked me up after the collapse of my first marriage and later, when I returned to the show, helped me cope when my mum was suffering from Alzheimer's. But I'd also laughed until I was crying and shared with them my most intimate and naughty secrets – sorry, Ray! Best of all, I'd had the privilege of interviewing some of the world's greatest stars.

People like Enrique Iglesias, who really must be the most beautiful man on the planet. Again, sorry, Ray! Enrique's been on several times and on each occasion I've turned into a giggling schoolgirl. He only needs to put his hand on my arm or flash his gorgeous smile and I melt. It was a close-run thing between Denise and me over who swooned more. I think I won that one.

I always loved it when we had really big stars on whom I've followed and admired for years. My favourite guest ever was Whoopi Goldberg. She was hilarious and not at all starry, as I'd feared she might be. When she was on, I couldn't believe I was sitting next to her and she was so nice. Despite being one of the most famous actresses in the world, she arrived without an entourage, went on just as she'd turned up and was brilliant. She was a complete contrast to the singer Rihanna, who turned up with about thirty people fussing around her. I thought, You've only come on to sing a three-minute song about an umbrella, love.

Yes, being on that panel had felt very special. I'd let the *Loose Women* audience into my life and now I was walking away from all that. Well, there's no going back now, I told myself.

After the announcement, time seemed to whiz by. Before I knew it, it was my last day as a Loose Woman. It felt a little bit like leaving school. You have your moments when you hate it and can't wait for your time there to end but as the big day gets closer you realize just how much you're going to miss it — and what a scary place is waiting for you outside.

'Please come with me on my last day. I need you there,' I told Ray. 'I think I'm going to be a bit of a mess and I'll need someone to mop me up and take me home afterwards.' Thank goodness, he promised he'd be with me every step of the way. And Jake wanted to come, too.

I couldn't look at anyone that morning, Thursday, 28 July, when we walked into ITV's South Bank studios. Everywhere I turned there were people who seemed sad to see me go. All the members of the team — the cameramen, the floor manager, the runners — seemed to be crying. Perhaps they were just being nice to me but they'd been my workmates for ten years and it certainly looked very genuine. I kept my eyes locked on the floor and hurried in quickly. It was too early in the day for them to set me off, too.

The producers had lined up a great last show, with

some of my all-time favourite panel members. The lovely Kate Thornton was anchor and my old friends Denise Welch and Sherrie Hewson were with me. I was glad to be among friends on my final day.

I settled myself into my seat behind the famous desk and felt the heat of the studio lights on my face. The audience was being thoroughly entertained by the warm-up man, and through my earpiece I could hear the directors singing, 'Don't Leave Me This Way'. Suddenly it hit me how much I was going to miss it all. That feeling came back again and I knew I was making a mistake. Keep it together, Nolan, I said to myself. Let's just get through the show somehow.

Then the familiar music was running and the show had begun. 'After ten years of laughter, tears and the odd verbal fisticuffs, today we say goodbye to a woman who is absolutely at the heart of the show,' said Kate. Well, that was all it took. I've never cried so much on national TV in my life.

'Don't even look at me!' I sobbed, searching for a hankie to blow my nose.

The team had planned all sorts of surprises. Half-naked men brought me chocolate pudding and I was given a (massive) nurse's dress to remind me of my naughty confession about Ray's fantasies in the bedroom! I was even presented with a star! The lovely production crew had registered a genuine one in my name. I loved that! I've framed the certificate for the Coleen Nova star and it now takes pride of place in my downstairs loo in Wilmslow.

Then it was time for the first guest. They'd thought long and hard about who to choose to send me on my way and I was thrilled to see the gorgeous *Torchwood* actor John Barrowman walking on set. He leaped on me and gave me a huge snog – much to the embarrassment of Ray and Jake, who were sitting in the studio audience. Later, John would somehow end up dancing around in the nurse's dress, which he enjoyed a little bit too much, if you ask me!

Then the brilliant comic Brian Conley, whom I'd known for years, waltzed on and serenaded me. 'You were my first true love, Coleen,' he declared. 'I wanted to elope with you, but you were only seventeen.' That made me laugh. It was the first I'd heard of it! Then he gave me a hug and ruined the sincerity of the moment by placing his hands on my breasts!

'If they had brains you'd be prime minister,' he said, to much uproar. We sang a duet, a version of Cole Porter's 'It's De-Lovely', which made everyone laugh because my part only consisted of singing 'de' every once in a while. Then we danced and hugged some more. It was lovely. By the time they ran the videotape of my best bits on the show I was an absolute mess.

Kate told me I had just one minute left as a Loose Woman and I could barely get my words out to say a last thank you. 'You girls will be my friends for ever so it's not goodbye,' I said. 'But I want to say a huge thank you to the audience at home who have been through my life with me for the past ten years. You've stood by me and made me what I am today. I'll probably get criticized for being too cheesy but I love each and every one of you.' And with that I was in tears again!

But I had one last surprise of my own. I'd decided I wanted my parting shot to be a musical one and I'd found a gorgeous Carole King song, 'Say Goodbye Today', which seemed to say everything I wanted to say to the girls and to the audience. Ray knew how nervous I was singing live in front of millions and, bless him, he'd promised to step up and play his guitar alongside me.

I made my way to the microphone and prayed my attempt to sing live would go a little better than it had in rehearsals, which had been a disaster. Thank God we'd decided to rehearse the song thoroughly because I was so nervous. While everyone else was off set I'd gone into the studio with our director Jo to give it a dry run. But as soon as I heard the soundtrack starting to play my breathing had gone completely bonkers and I couldn't sing a note. Not one note. Lovely, patient Jo went, 'OK, we'll go again.' But it was no good. No matter how hard I tried I couldn't get the first few lines out without breaking down into floods of tears. I could hear her voice saying patiently, 'You'll be fine, don't worry,' but it was just making me worse! Anyway, God love her, she made me try it about ten times until I was so used to it I managed to fight my way through the entire song. If it hadn't have been for her I wouldn't have managed one note on the day.

So, now I had to do it for real, live on TV. I stepped out from behind the desk and walked over to the stage.

Taking hold of the mic, I managed to whisper, 'I'm scared. I apologize!' before launching into the words of the song, which I'd changed slightly to suit the moment.

'Say goodbye today', I sang, with tears streaming down my face.

By the time the last notes faded I was sobbing like a baby! I genuinely felt sad. I know why it hit me so hard: it was because I love *Loose Women*. It's like 'I'm In The Mood For Dancing'. I could never knock either of those things because both of them helped to make me who I am today. Whatever I do in life it will always be that show and that song that people identify me with. And that's just fine by me.

The end credits ran and before I knew it we were off air. I really was no longer a Loose Woman. The cast and the crew went out together for a boozy lunch that lasted way too long and left me feeling tired and even more emotional! Pissed, in other words. I don't drink a lot and it's usually me telling the others off for over-doing it, but on that occasion I was leading the way. I even managed to keep up with Denise!

On the train home with Ray and Jake I thought about all the things that *Loose Women* had given me. Good friends, amazing experiences, encounters with some of my greatest heroes, a steady income and an incredible feeling of safety and security. It seemed impossible that I was closing that particular door for ever.

Still, it was exciting knowing that, with only two days a week in London on the Hub for *This Morning*, I could enjoy more time with Ciara and focus on my marriage. And, with Bernie most definitely on the up, it seemed life was finally back on track. But I couldn't shake the feeling that I might have made a huge mistake in leaving *Loose Women*. I couldn't put my finger on it but I had a feeling that it might not be the end. And, deep down, I really hoped it wasn't. I had to leave but I really hoped that somehow, one day, I might be able to return.

# Chapter Six

What happened to me next remains one of the most harrowing and upsetting experiences of my life. Was it a coincidence? A lucky guess by a passing stranger? Or something genuinely spiritual? Who knows? Whatever it was, the day began with a lovely walk along a beautiful beach in LA, and ended with a little old lady in a headscarf delivering the news that was to bring my happy life crashing down.

After *Loose Women* had ended I found I had much more time on my hands. I spoke to Ray and Ciara, and we decided it was about time we treated ourselves to a family holiday. We certainly needed one. What with the stress of the rows with Ray, the constant trips to London for work and the worry over Bernie, the thought of lying on a beach or next to a swimming-pool with nothing to think about but which paperback to read next was very appealing.

We're not usually up for exotic, far-flung destinations. You'll never see paparazzi pictures of me and Ray cavorting on a tropical beach or diving off a yacht – chance would be a fine thing! We're more likely to choose somewhere closer to home. Somewhere in Europe perhaps or, more likely, a British seaside resort. My agent Neil's always telling me to spend some money but I'm just not built that way – I like my tea and my cornflakes and my other home comforts! But, after such a busy time and all the recent heartache, we decided to splash out and take a trip to America.

There were six of us going. Me, Ray and Ciara, our dear friends Nick and Paul, and Laura, another mate who would come to do a bit of babysitting for us. Excitedly, we sat around the kitchen table and drew up a list of all the famous places we wanted to see.

'New York!'

'No, Texas!'

'How about Boston?'

Nick and Paul had spent a lot of time in California and lobbied for that. With its beaches and gorgeous scenery, it would be perfect for us, they said. Plus it had all the glamour of Hollywood, with its studios and film-star houses, to keep us busy. Eventually we decided on a week in Las Vegas and a week in Los Angeles. When we told Ciara she was so excited. She couldn't wait to get to the USA and drove us all mad by counting down how many sleeps there were before we could go.

Just before we left, I heard from Bernie that she was worried about a lump she'd found on the left side of her chest. We were all desperately afraid that it signalled the return of the cancer but the thought was so horrendous I think we kind of buried it. We'd got used to the idea that Bernie was going to be fine. Anne and Linda had remained clear after their treatment: surely Bernie would kick it too.

'I'm cancelling the trip,' I told Linda, the day after I heard the news. 'There's no way I'm going so far away, knowing Bernie might be ill again.'

But when it got back to Bernie, she insisted that we went. She wasn't panicking, she said. Her next mammogram for her natural breast was due in a fortnight's time and she'd decided to wait until then to have the new lump looked at.

'I'm sure it's fine. By the time you get home I'll have been told it's nothing,' she said – bravely, I now realize. 'For Christ's sake, go and have a great holiday and stop bloody worrying.'

Bernie could be quite fierce when she wanted to be – she wouldn't entertain darker thoughts and she didn't want the rest of us dwelling on them either. So we decided to do as we were told and have our American adventure after all.

'One more sleep, Ciara!' I said, the night before we flew. 'Get ready to meet some cowboys!'

The next day the six of us excitedly checked into Manchester airport and waited at the departure gate for our plane. It was a long old flight but Ciara couldn't have been happier, watching DVDs and hoovering up the free crisps and goodie bags. The moment we landed at McCarran International Airport there was no doubting we were in Las Vegas. Even in the airport there were slot machines and roulette wheels – it was mad but thrilling! Las Vegas itself was so big and bright and everything was on a massive scale.

As a special treat, we'd booked ourselves in at the

impressive Encore, a luxury hotel and casino that is said to be one of the best in the world. When we saw our fabulous bedrooms we were like excited schoolkids. I was in love with the spas and the glamorous shops, and the boys were always heading off to the swimming-pool, with its private cabanas, complete with fridge and plasma TV! Ciara was in her element, eating huge pizzas and hanging out with the adults.

It was good to be away with Nick and Paul. Ray and I had met them through work in the north-west and we had clicked immediately. We've become really close over the years and they're hilarious, as well as being genuinely lovely people. They'd stayed in Vegas lots of times and knew all the great places to go. What made me laugh, though, was that as soon as we landed Nick immediately turned into an American and started calling us all 'sweetie' or 'dude'.

'If you call your mobile a cell phone one more time I'll toss it into that bloody swimming-pool!' I joked.

Having been born and raised in Blackpool, I was used to the sound of slot machines and amusement arcades. As soon as I walked down the famous Strip it was like I was five again, being taken by my mum and dad to the Golden Mile. Seeing so many people posting their dimes into fruit machines was fun at first but, unlike Blackpool, in Vegas you just couldn't get away from it. There were machines everywhere – as soon as you stepped into our lovely hotel, you could hear them in the lobby. To be honest, I'd had enough by the end of our stay.

The highlight of our Vegas trip was a cowboy-trail horse ride into the Red Rock Canyon conservation area. Ciara, Laura, Ray and I went out with this real-life cowboy, who led us into the most amazing scenery. With the red mountains, deep canyons and prickly cactus all around, it was just like being in an old John Wayne film. We barbecued steak under the stars and toasted marshmallows over the fire. It was blissful and I hope Ciara will remember it for the rest of her life.

The next day we drove four and a half hours to Los Angeles for the final leg of our holiday. Nick and Paul had recommended the glorious Mondrian boutique hotel on Sunset Boulevard in West Hollywood. Oh, my God, it was gorgeous – even better than our Vegas hotel. This time there was a rooftop pool and lounge area with panoramic views of LA. At night, they'd put hundreds of flickering lanterns on the deck around the pool. It was so Hollywood! Next to the swimming-pool is the Mondrian's famous Skybar, a regular haunt of film stars and movie executives. Everywhere was super-posh and I kept expecting to bump into somebody really famous. The best we did was spotting the England football players, who had just checked in when we arrived.

We sunbathed, swam, ate and took a few tours around Hollywood. From time to time my stomach would flip and I'd wonder how Bernie was, praying that by now she'd had the all-clear. Although we were doing our best to have a good time on holiday, Bernie was never far from my mind.

We wanted to spend some time by the sea so after a few days we drove to Venice Beach. It's a crazy place and everywhere you look there are musicians, jugglers, acrobats and other circus acts trying to grab your attention. We were walking along the boardwalk, which runs at the back of the beach, when Nick suddenly spotted a sign for a fortune-teller, who was supposedly quite famous, a wizened old woman who was said to be spookily accurate.

'Come with me, Col,' he begged. 'It's only twenty dollars and we'll have a laugh.'

'You've got to be kidding,' I said. 'It's probably a man with a tea towel wrapped around his head. I'm from Blackpool, remember? I've seen it all before.'

When it comes to that sort of hocus-pocus, I've always been somebody who sat on the fence. I'd love to believe that Tarot cards and tea leaves and crystal balls really can help you see into the future but that's impossible, isn't it? Ray's even more adamant. To him it's all a load of complete cobblers and, typical York-shireman, he's too tight to spend money on stuff like that.

'It's just a load of rubbish, count me out,' he said. Paul was firmly in Ray's court and Ciara wanted to have her hair braided so off they went to find the braid-ing stall.

Nick looked at me appealingly with puppy-dog eyes, his palms slapped together as if in prayer. 'Oh, go on, then.' I laughed. 'But she'll just talk nonsense, I'm telling you.'

The fortune-teller looked ancient and incredibly small – she must have been in her eighties at least – and was sitting at a table under a parasol to protect her from the sun. Around her head she wore a red scarf with little silver discs that jingled like bells with every tiny movement. She was draped in a marvellous robe covered with swirls of purple, scarlet and gold. It was enormous and swamped her small frame. The table in front of her was laid with a crimson cloth, and a set of Tarot cards was stacked neatly by her side, waiting to reveal their secrets. How the bloody hell did I let myself get talked into this? I thought.

Nick wanted to go first. The old woman seemed to go on for ever so I wandered off along the boardwalk to watch the other acts. A fire-eater was swallowing great balls of flame and, a bit further on, a juggler appeared to be throwing at least ten oranges into the air and catching them one by one. People were out enjoying the Californian sunshine, roller-skating and walking their dogs.

Suddenly Nick was running after me to tell me it was my turn. 'She's amazing, Coleen,' he said. 'She's just told me I had an admirer and that I'm going to cross some water.'

'That'll be the hotel waiter who keeps giving you the eye.' I laughed. 'And as for crossing water, you don't need to be a gypsy to know that. You've got an English accent, you dick!'

I have to admit I was hugely sceptical. I've had my fortune told many times before but at home I often suspect that I'm just about well known enough – especially in Blackpool – for the person to have read about me in the newspapers. Hang on, you could have just Googled that, I always think. But in LA I was totally anonymous: nobody knew a thing about me. If this woman came up with anything interesting it would be a miracle.

I sat down opposite her and watched her timeworn hands begin to throw Tarot characters on to the table. I had no idea what any of the cards meant but the results were obviously agitating her. She'd deal them, study them intently and shake her head, the tiny silver discs dancing frantically about and making a tinkling sound.

After a few minutes she swept the cards up again. 'I need to shuffle them,' she told me, and her ancient brow creased even more deeply. She was muttering something under her breath and I was starting to think Ray had been right to avoid her. She dealt the cards once again.

'I need to ask if you're all right,' she said.

I told her I was. 'As far as I know!' I joked, but my laughter fell silently on to the table.

Then she said, 'Someone really close to you isn't all right. Is it your sister?'

I felt my stomach do a little flip, my mouth went dry and I nodded slowly.

Encouraged, she went on: 'I'm so sorry but it's come back and there's nothing the doctors can do.'

By now she was manically turning the cards over.

'I'm trying to find a good card, honestly I am, but I can't alter what they're telling me. They say the next eighteen months are going to be awful. Your sister will be strong and courageous and fight it to the end – but she will not win.'

I could feel myself getting angry. You can piss right off here and now, I thought. I don't want to hear this. It's a load of rubbish, just like Ray warned it would be. But I was asking myself how this woman could possibly know. I hadn't breathed a word to her about Bernie and here she was telling me that I was going to lose her.

'Your husband is going to be amazing. He'll support you every step of the way but he'll fall apart when she dies,' she continued. 'I don't know what you do for a living but you're working on something soon for a lot of money. It won't lead to what you hoped for, and it will be a hard year, but after that justice will prevail. Does that make any sense to you?'

I couldn't answer her, I was so distressed. I just stood up, knocking my chair over, and ran off to find Nick.

When he saw my face he was worried. 'God, Col, you look like you've seen a ghost,' he said. 'What happened with the fortune-teller?'

I couldn't speak. I just muttered something about it getting late and needing to find Ciara and Ray so we set off for the hair-braiding stall.

When I found Ray I pulled him to one side to tell him what the old woman had said. His face clouded and he was instantly fuming. 'Forget it,' he stormed. 'She hasn't got a clue.' But on the forty-five-minute drive back to the hotel I couldn't shake the feeling of dread. I had a horrible suspicion that the woman had somehow genuinely known what Fate had in store for my family. Friends have since told me that a good psychic would never predict bad news like that. I've no idea why she chose to do so that day.

At ten o'clock the next morning my phone rang as I was having breakfast alongside the hotel pool. It was Neil. I knew he wouldn't normally call me on holiday unless it was absolutely necessary, so I guessed whatever it was must be important. Instinctively, I left our table and found a shady bit of the open rooftop restaurant. I could see the traffic below, moving like tiny model cars down the busy boulevard.

'Hi, it's me,' he said gently. 'I'm so sorry to call while you're away but I'm afraid I've got to tell you something in case it leaks out and you hear it second hand. The girls wanted to wait until you got home but I knew you'd want to know as soon as I did . . .' He trailed off as if to give me a second to prepare myself for what he was about to say.

My stomach made the same little flip as it had done the day before. 'Oh god, what is it?' I said.

I could hear him take a deep breath and then he said softly, 'There's no easy way to say this but Bernie has had some terrible news.'

I felt my breath leave my body as I clutched the phone.

'The latest test results are back,' he continued. 'I'm so sorry, Coleen, but the cancer is back and it's really not good.'

'How bad is it?' I managed to ask, barely able to hold on to the phone.

'It's as bad as it could have been. The doctors have told her it's spread to her lungs, liver, bones and brain. They're going to put her on medication and she's amazingly positive. I really am so sorry to be telling you this but I knew you would want to know right away.'

Oh my god, my mind raced trying to take in the devastating news.

*It had spread to her brain and her bones, her brain and her bones* . . . I remember repeating those words over and over again. It was just too awful.

Back in Britain it was only two in the morning: Neil had stayed up late rather than waking me too early with the news. I thanked him for telling me – he was right, it would have been awful to hear it from anyone else. I understood why my sisters had wanted to wait but I definitely needed to know. I was immediately desperate to speak to Bernie, but somehow I managed to hold off for another six hours before it was morning in the UK. With shaky hands, I dialled her number. She answered the phone and it was obvious I'd woken her. 'Oh, you've heard,' she said, her voice sounding a long, long way away. 'Well, listen, it's absolutely fine. It's not curable but it's treatable. The doctors are going to blast it with drugs and it's going to be OK. They said they've had patients with similar diagnoses who have still been around fourteen or fifteen years down the line.'

As Neil had said, she was just so positive. Of all us girls, Bernie had always been the optimist. There was never a moment that she moaned she was dying from cancer. Her philosophy was that she was living with it. And on that day, as she was explaining to me all the changes that were taking place in her body, it was Bernie who was comforting me and saying that everything was going to be fine.

I listened to her talking about how people had lived long lives with this stage of cancer. I so wanted to believe her, I desperately wanted to feel the optimism I felt the first time she was diagnosed, but all I could think of was the bloody fortune-teller with her cards. I could hear her predict that Bernie would have no more than eighteen months to live and I was thinking, No, it's not going to be fine. It's not going to be fine at all.

I haven't told too many people this story because I know they'll think I've exaggerated or even made it up. But I really haven't, I promise. I wouldn't go back to the woman on the beach for a million pounds. From now on I don't want to know what's in store for me, good or bad.

Ray had taken Ciara off so that I could make the call home. Once I'd found him, he could see at once that

I'd had bad news. I wish now that I'd never told him about the fortune-teller's prediction because, of course, he knew to expect the worst. We couldn't put the genie back in the bottle: our innocence had been shattered for ever. It shook his absolute conviction about 'mumbo-jumbo hocus-pocus' to the core. We knew we had to keep the truth from Ciara and the rest of our little holiday family so we put on happy faces and somehow got through the rest of our American jaunt.

By the time we arrived back in the UK the rest of my brothers and sisters had been told Bernie's news. I don't think you could say that any one of us was more upset than the rest but I know my brother Brian, who lived near a few of the girls in Blackpool, took it very badly.

'You need to look out for Brian up there,' said Bernie, from her home in Weybridge. 'I've told him it's all going to be OK and that the doctors are going to blast the cancer with drugs, but he's struggling.' It was typical of her that she was more concerned for others.

Bernie made us all take an oath of secrecy. She was touring with a production of *Chicago*, wowing audiences as the no-nonsense lesbian prison matron Mama Morton, and she wanted to carry on doing it. Nobody who saw her on stage that year belting out 'When You're Good To Mama' would have guessed the truth. Every three weeks Bernie would go back to the Royal

Surrey Hospital for blood tests and to get a drip to strengthen her bones, but apart from those days she never missed a single performance. The truth was, she needed to work in order to carry on feeling like Bernie. We were all so desperately worried about her being on the road and away from her family but nobody wanted to take that from her.

I texted her once to see how she was coping. *Don't you think you should tell the show that you're ill?* I said. *Perhaps you should be resting at home instead.*

Her defiant reply came through almost instantly. *What am I going to do if I don't work?* she wrote. *Sit around the house feeling like Cancer Girl?* I'm not sure I agreed with her, but I had to admit she was certainly courageous.

Meanwhile I was still working at *This Morning*, looking after the Hub interaction section of the show. With Bernie so much on my mind I was beginning to feel increasingly unhappy about working away from home and I was missing my own family. Bernie's illness had certainly put everything into perspective. Plus, it was hard to be in an environment where I couldn't discuss the one topic that was uppermost in my mind. With Bernie insisting that we kept her illness private, I had nobody to talk to about it when things got tough at work. I've always found that it helps to talk about what's bothering you and I hated not being able to share my fears.

Once again there was an announcement about my leaving – but this time I couldn't reveal the real reason for my decision. I did quite a few interviews at the time, where I'd talk about missing the family and needing a rest. Of Bernie and her ever-worsening condition, I said nothing.

On my last day on set I was genuinely sorry to be leaving. But what is it with me and goodbyes? That final show proved to be a complete and utter sob-fest! Phil gave me a massive hug and Holly surprised me with the largest bouquet of flowers ever. 'We're really going to miss you,' she said.

I hadn't expected to be so upset, but before I knew it I was sobbing into the camera. Looking back on it now, I think I was very stressed about things back home. My worries for Bernie and the fact I couldn't talk to anyone at work about her illness had made the situation far more emotional.

'I've had the best two years ever. Honestly I feel really sad,' I wailed. 'Don't get me to talk a lot, but thank you for making me part of the whole family. It really is like that here, especially with the crew and people behind the scenes.'

After we went off air I had a few drinks with the crew and packed my one or two belongings into a suitcase. A taxi arrived to take me to Euston station and that was it. I was leaving *This Morning* again.

As the Manchester train rushed along the track I could feel my anxiety easing. Every single mile I put between London and Wilmslow seemed to make another knot of tension vanish. I watched as canals and fields and tiny back gardens of terraced houses flashed past the window and just hoped upon hope that Bernie would be around for a long time to see such ordinary scenes. I was glad to call time on my TV work for a while, but I still felt so very sad.

That summer I was able to spend time at home with Ciara, Ray and, when they were there, the boys. It was good to have a rest and it felt important to have my family around me. Ciara and I spent hours down at the stables, looking after her pony, Paddy. By now we'd bought a second horse, Orla, a big dark Irish draught-cross-thoroughbred for me to ride. It had been my childhood dream to have one and, although it had taken me almost thirty-five years to get one, I'd done it at last.

Having Orla changed our lives. It meant that Ciara and I could ride and spend lots of quality mother-daughter time together. We'd looked at Horsemart online, or something similar, and Orla was the first we'd gone to see. As soon as I saw her I thought, Jesus, she's big. But, to be fair, she was probably looking at me and thinking the same thing! People think you're loaded if you have a horse but she cost something like five hundred pounds. The upkeep is the expensive thing, but Ciara and I do most of it ourselves.

Our typical rainy British summer continued and Bernie was never far from my mind. We'd text every day and she'd keep me up to date with news of her hospital appointments. Sometimes she sounded down, at other times you'd hardly know there was anything wrong. I kept reminding her she had a strong support network of brothers and sisters up north waiting to drop everything and dash down to Surrey if she needed us.

The one thing that had shaken Bernie most was when the doctors told her that the cancer had spread to her brain. It totally terrified her. She said she felt as if there was some alien thing inside her that could, at any moment, take away the essence of who she was.

She had admitted to Erin that the cancer had returned, but she'd not been able to tell her just how advanced it was. Now the doctors were giving her a cocktail of really strong drugs to keep it at bay. There was no more chemo at this stage, just a nasty dose of oral medicine that she coped with bravely. Her consultant arranged for her to have regular scans, which somehow she fitted around her gruelling work schedule. Once the results came through Bernie would feed them back to the rest of the family. If the house phone rang I'd jump out of my skin. In our family we tend to keep in touch by text so I was always worried it could only mean more bad news.

One day Bernie rang me. 'Who are you with?' she asked. I didn't like the sound of this at all – it was too much like the time she'd phoned to tell me she was ill.

'I'm with Ray and the kids, why?' I said. 'What's happened, Bernie?'

'Are you sitting down?' she asked. By now I was convinced it was very bad news indeed. 'Because I need to tell you, the cancer has totally gone from my brain!'

Well, they must have heard me screaming all the way to Manchester. I was so delighted, it was like I'd won the lottery. Ray ran into the kitchen to see what was going on and found me dancing around the breakfast bar, punching the air.

'The doctors can't explain why, but the cancer's gone from my brain!' Bernie was saying again. 'And they reckon it's shrunk quite a lot everywhere else!' It was the news we'd been praying for. The treatment was having an effect!

Could we dare to hope that it would go on working and save our sister? I resolved to push the dire warnings of the Venice Beach fortune-teller out of my head completely. While Bernie was being positive, and her doctors were being reassuring, why should I believe a crazy woman? Miracles could happen, it seemed.

'Bernie, that's the best news I've ever heard,' I told her. 'You're going to beat this!'

Cautious optimism set in and I no longer jumped quite so much when the telephone rang. It made me think that perhaps life could get back to normal and I could start thinking about a short telly project that would pay well enough to let me stay at home a little while longer.

It was around this time that I had the first hint of my next bit of drama. The way this business works, you often get called in for talks with producers about future TV shows. Generally, you go in, meet the people in charge, get excited about the job – and never hear from them again. So when Neil told me the producers of *Celebrity Big Brother* wanted to have a chat I didn't really think it would lead to much.

I hoped that it would, though! I'm an absolute *Big Brother* nut. I've watched that programme since day one – the ordinary *BB* and the celeb version – and I'm always totally hooked. I love seeing how the experience plays with the minds of the housemates – but I also know that the celebrity version can kill a career if things don't go well.

The previous series of *Celebrity Big Brother* had run that January and my former *Loose Women* partner in crime Denise Welch was fresh out of the house. She'd had quite a time in there – some pretty big highs and terrible lows – and had eventually emerged victorious as the winner. Nevertheless she warned me off.

'Until you're in there and at the mercy of Big Brother's mind games you have no idea what it's like,' she told me, when I revealed I was thinking about having talks with the show's producers. 'Honestly, Col, it's no wonder people go in and find it so tough.'

She was speaking from experience. Denise had hated her time on the show, largely because she felt she was bullied by a number of her fellow housemates. There were rows and a bit of tipsy behaviour and things had got out of hand. Ray and I had watched every episode and felt very uncomfortable for her – especially the night she stripped off in the hot tub and flashed her boobs to the nation. Once she was out she discovered what people had been saying about her and the fuss that Jacuzzigate had caused. She was very upset. But Denise's life was totally different from mine. I knew she had issues before she went in – her marriage was in trouble and she was drinking too much. She also had a continuing problem with depression and who knew how that would pan out in a house full of strangers, away from her loved ones? I was worried at the thought of her going on the show, but it wasn't my place to say. Besides, the large amount of money they offer you is ridiculous!

I knew that *Celebrity Big Brother* would pay me enough money to stay at home with Ciara for a year. I'd finished *This Morning* and *Loose Women* and I really, really wanted to take a year off. To be honest, I didn't think I had it in me any longer to go to work and be funny on TV. It seemed a bit weird to crack jokes when my sister was battling for her life. But I'd spoken to Bernie and she didn't want the public to know. She was trying to protect Erin, who wasn't yet aware of the full extent of her disease, and to keep things as normal as possible for as long as possible.

Money aside, the thought of being in the *CBB* line-up was scary. And, yes, I was terrified of being cut off from my family and away from home for three and a half weeks, or however long I would be in there. But I knew Ciara, who was also a big fan, would be beside herself with excitement at the thought of watching her mum in the *Big Brother* house. It was Ray's reaction

I was more concerned about. He and I had sat through enough series to know that housemates are at the mercy of the producer's edit.

'You won't have any say about how they show you, you know, Col,' he warned. 'They could make you out to be a complete bitch and you wouldn't know a thing about it until you came out the other side.'

He was right, of course. But after a long night discussing the pros and cons, we both agreed it was one of those chance-in-a-lifetime opportunities that was too good to turn down.

I called Neil the next morning. 'Let's meet them,' I said. 'It can't hurt to just talk, can it?'

We travelled down to London and met with the executives of Channel 5, which had taken over the running of the show. The people involved seemed really nice and I had to go through all sorts of tests and sit through a few interviews to make sure I was right for the programme. 'Oh, well, that's the last I'll hear of that,' I said to Neil, as we left the offices.

A few weeks passed and I began to think it had been a fuss about nothing. I was sure they would have chosen their housemates by now and I was a little relieved not to be going in. What had I been thinking of? I'd been mad to imagine I could leave Ciara and Ray and spend more than three weeks with a bunch of strangers, living my life on national TV.

Then one day my mobile rang and it was Neil. 'I hope you've got some nice pyjamas,' he said cryptically.

'Err . . . yes, I have, but why on earth are you asking me that?' I asked him, laughing at the absurdity of the question. I could almost hear him smiling on the other end of the line when he spoke next.

'Because you're going to be locked up in an extremely famous house with a crowd of people you've never met before!'

I immediately felt sick with worry and full of excitement all at the same time. Oh. My. God. I was going into *Big Brother*! And I had absolutely no idea what was about to hit me . . .

# Chapter Seven

I was allowed to take just one suitcase into the *Big Brother* house. And for me the choice of what to put in there was easy. Knickers. And even more knickers. I knew there wouldn't be anywhere to wash my clothes and that I needed to pack enough clean underwear for a possible three-and-a-half-week stay, so in went twenty-five pairs of brand-new knickers. Even if I get chucked out on the first vote, at least I'll have some nice new pants, I thought. After that, it was a case of throwing in a couple of eviction-night outfits and enough casual clothes to see me through.

Suitcase packed, I sat in the living room with Ray and Ciara waiting for the car to collect me and take me down south. The *CBB* experience is amazing: it's run like a military operation. The producers want to keep the identity of the contestants secret until the moment they walk into the house and they do it by hiding them for two days beforehand in a hotel close to the studios. It gives them time to film all the pre-entry interviews and stops the housemates reading too much in the papers about who they're likely to be living with. But it means two days in isolation, and I knew that as soon as I left my own house and family it could be almost a month before I spoke to them again.

Ciara is a *Big Brother* fan and was excited about me taking part, so she was fine. I sat in my kitchen watching her chatter away, trying to soak up as much of her as I could. Ray was trying to be upbeat but I could tell he was worried. I filled in the silences between us by running through all the domestic jobs that would need doing while I was away.

'Don't forget that Ciara needs new school shoes before September,' I burbled on. 'There's a supermarket delivery arriving on Friday and you'll need dog food before that.' We have two ancient golden cocker spaniels, Jessie, who is eleven, and Rio, who is twelve.

Then the doorbell rang and it was time to go. 'Be good for Dad and make sure you watch me!' I told Ciara, as I hugged and kissed her for the millionth time.

Ray was quiet. 'Take care and don't let them make you do anything you don't want to do,' he said. Much to the embarrassment of Ciara, we had quite a long snog on the doorstep. Then Ray added, 'Just be yourself and you'll be fine.'

I stepped into the car and lowered the window. 'See you in the diary room!' I said, waving frantically.

I'd thought the big goodbye would be more emotional but, as I left Wilmslow, I felt just like I was going off to work. I'm used to travelling down to London each week and leaving Ray and Ciara wasn't so bad. It was only when we were getting closer to the hotel a few hours later that I began to feel a bit wobbly.

The car wound its way through the Hertfordshire countryside and eventually pulled up outside a smart hotel called the Village. The driver helped me out and fetched my suitcase and I wandered into Reception to find a nice, smiling girl who, it turned out, would not leave my side for the next forty-eight hours.

'Hi, Coleen, I'm Sarah and I'm your chaperone,' she said, holding out her hand. 'I'm going to show you to your room but, first things first, can you give me your mobile, please?'

'Sorry? Why do you need that?' I asked. I'm a bit wedded to my phone and felt slightly panicky at the thought of being separated from it. Giving up my phone felt like playing right into the programme makers' hands.

'Don't worry, it's just our normal procedure,' said Sarah. 'We want to make sure you don't speak to any-body in the outside world before you go into the *Big Brother* house.'

I handed the phone over obediently. It felt odd, but it was just the start of the weirdness. For the next two days I wasn't allowed to leave my hotel bedroom. I had to eat, sleep and live in there, chaperoned constantly by Sarah. It's a very strange thing to be so close for so long to somebody you have only just met but she was lovely and, by the end of our time together, I felt quite attached to her. The poor girl must have been bored out of her mind looking after me, though. Apart from going to the room next door to sleep, she never let me out of her sight.

'Night, Coleen,' she'd say, before going over to the bedroom phone, unplugging it and taking it with her.

When Room Service knocked on the door to deliver my meals I had to dive into the en suite bathroom. They didn't even want the staff to see who was in the hotel, just in case they ran downstairs to tell everyone who was going to be on the show. The other house-mates were also guests, of course, but we never had a chance to bump into one another. Even when you checked out and left, you had a cloak thrown over your head! It was like being on a secret mission.

*Big Brother* always debrands your clothes so you don't go into the house as a walking advertisement. Everything has to have its label unpicked or covered with gaffer tape – it took me and Sarah hours. 'I can do this, you don't need to,' she kept saying. But, to be honest, I was glad of the distraction. What else was I going to do? Being locked inside a hotel room for two days without talking to anyone in the outside world is enough to drive me mad.

I really didn't know who I'd be sharing the house with. You hear and read rumours about likely contest-ants, but until you walk down those stairs you really don't know anything for sure. The rumour mill had it that *Coronation Street* icon Julie Goodyear and Spandau Ballet's Martin Kemp were going in, which was very exciting. Julie's character Bet Lynch is an absolute legend and Martin Kemp had been a guest on *Loose Women* so I knew I already loved him. Lots of really good friends – people whose judgement I trust – had warned me that Julie could be difficult. But I was deter-mined not to go in with any preconceptions. 'We're both northern, we both like a laugh, it'll be fine,' I told myself.

By Wednesday, 15 August, my nervous wait was over and the day had come to leave the hotel and enter the house. There were to be thirteen of us and I was the eleventh to go in. By the time I arrived, ten celebrities were already in the house and getting to know one another. I stood at the doors of the studio, two very sexy men wearing nothing but tiny black shorts and a dicky bow at my side, waiting to step outside and walk towards the host Brian Dowling. I still didn't know who was inside the house but I'd heard the jeers and whistles thrown at them from the audience. I prayed I wouldn't be booed and, thank God, the crowd was lovely and gave me a great reception. 'I'm so frightened!' I told Brian truthfully. But there was no going back now. Brian wished me luck, the famous doors opened in front of me and I took a deep breath. Then I stepped inside.

The first person I saw was Julie Goodyear. She was wearing her signature leopard print – leopard and bright pink tights and a pair of leopard cat's ears. Her T-shirt said 'Get It. Got It. Good.' That's telling us, I thought. Also there, to my absolute delight, was Cheryl Fergison, who played Heather in *EastEnders*. I'd met Cheryl on *Loose Women* and *This Morning* and I knew she was hilarious. We'd always got on. I laughed as soon as I saw her and didn't stop until she was evicted. Then there was Julian Clary, who has the sort of face that cracks me up without him having to say anything.

He looks at you and you know what he's thinking – and it's usually very rude! Finally, I spotted MC Harvey, who had been a member of So Solid Crew and was already a friend through Antony Costa from Blue. Antony and I are very close, I always call him my celebrity child, and I knew if he liked Harvey, then I would, too.

But I didn't have a clue who the other contestants were. I just saw this sea of faces looking up at me as I walked down the stairs. I kept hoping to spot an absolute Hollywood legend and, to be honest, I was a little disappointed. In previous years *Celebrity Big Brother* has usually signed up some massive American superstar. There was a rumour that Dog the Bounty Hunter – oh, my God, I love him! – was going to be in but he was nowhere to be seen. I read later the UK government refused to give him a visa because of his involvement in a murder almost forty years ago. I was gutted.

The sea of faces turned out to be someone called the Situation (who was on an American reality show called *Jersey Shore*), page-three model Rhian Sugden, Prince Lorenzo (drop-dead gorgeous but don't ask me what he does), Danica Thrall (a beautiful girl who had been on a show called *Sex, Lies & Rinsing Guys* in which she chatted up men on the Internet in return for presents) and Ashley McKenzie, bless him. Unlike everybody else, Ashley didn't have an ounce of ego and went around that first night saying, 'I bet you don't even know who I am, do you?' He is actually an

Olympian judo star and had just been competing in London 2012 but he hadn't been touched by the cynical side of showbiz. He was so sweet.

Also there was Samantha Brick, an outspoken, outrageous *Daily Mail* journalist. When I realized who she was I thought at once that we wouldn't get on. She's written ridiculous things in the past about being unpopular with other women because she's too attractive. Then there were the articles about how she felt a woman's place was in the home, cooking, cleaning and basically fawning all over her husband. I remember showing one of the pieces to Ray and laughing, 'In your dreams!' From her articles I thought we'd be chalk and cheese but Samantha turned out to be the sweetest person. She wouldn't thank me for saying so but she's nothing like her supposed character.

As I stepped into the house, I heard Julian say sweetly, 'Oh, look, there's a very famous woman coming down the stairs.' I almost looked behind me to see who he was talking about! It felt as if everybody in the room rushed over to offer air kisses and make me feel welcome. All except one person.

Julie Goodyear greeted me with a very different tone from Julian's. I'd been there thirty seconds when she announced loudly, 'Oh, here she is, the nation's favourite,' and walked towards me with her arms out. I'd never met the woman. I thought, What a weird thing to say. Straight away my guard went up and I knew immediately that I had a problem. I couldn't help feeling that she was being entirely false with me from the start.

Once inside, I was followed by glamour girl Jasmine Lennard, who in 2005 had been a finalist in the reality show *Make Me a Supermodel*. She sounded quite posh, oozed confidence and was incredible-looking. I bet she hasn't packed twenty-five pairs of M&S knickers, I thought.

The final housemate was Martin Kemp, who walked down those stairs looking every inch the handsome pop star. When we were rehearsing for our tour, Spandau Ballet had been working in the studio next to us. The girls and I would keep making excuses to bump into members of the group and Martin had always been especially lovely.

Things kicked off dramatically when Cheryl and Julie began an argument, which ended, to my horror, in Julie throwing a drink over Cheryl's head. I was puzzled. From what I knew of Cheryl she was the last person to stir up trouble. What was going on? I hate an unpleasant atmosphere so I tried to play the peacemaker, comforting Cheryl and telling Julie she shouldn't be wasting alcohol by chucking drinks around on the first night. Little did I know that Big Brother had set us all up – Cheryl and Julie had been told to act as drama queens and have a blazing row. They passed the challenge and won us a soap-opera party in the back garden!

It was a beautiful summer's evening and, with bubbles in our glasses and the prospect of making new and interesting friends, I began to relax and enjoy the experience. Julie and I sat together smoking and chatting away happily. Perhaps she's not so bad, I thought. I tried hard to make friends with her and hoped that being northern and having a similar sarcastic sense of humour would seal the deal.

Later, Big Brother opened up the bedroom and we chose our beds. I remember lying there that first night thinking, Oh, my God, there is going to be a camera on me first thing in the morning. How hideous. I barely let my family see me in that state, never mind the entire nation. It really was weird. I was in a bedroom with twelve complete strangers. I hadn't even had a cup of tea with them and here I was in my nightie.

We were given one small drawer each. When I've watched the show in the past, I've often wondered why housemates left their belongings on the floor – I know they're locked in a house but there's no need to be so revoltingly untidy, I thought. Now I realize it's all part of Big Brother's mind games. They want you to feel out of your comfort zone, which means making you drape your undies over the end of your bed. Similarly, I'd wondered why contestants wore sunglasses or a night mask in the bedroom. Now I know it's because the studio lights burn your eyes. You go from pitch black to full glare – it's horrendous, and such a rude awakening. For me, though, the lights were a reminder that we were in a studio and this was work. That knowledge stopped me being homesick for a while.

I've heard some past housemates saying that you forget you're being filmed, but that's just crap. You always know you're in a studio and that cameras are on you. What happens is that after a while you just stop caring.

Julie Goodyear was behaving very strangely towards me. Over the next few days she must have told me hundreds of times how much she loved me, but I couldn't shake off the suspicion that she was setting me up in some way. She was so sycophantic and fake. She loved everything about me, she said. She loved every piece of work I'd ever done; she loved my jewellery, my hair, my clothes. The other girls, Jasmine, Danica and Rhian, had brought beautiful designer gear into the house and Julie was loving mine from Primark and M&S! You can't possibly love me, I thought. It's one thing to say you enjoy watching someone's performance on TV, it's another to claim to be their number-one fan.

But then I watched her and I realized she was doing the same thing to everybody else. She would be sickly sweet and then, as soon as their back was turned, she would slag them off. With the younger ones, she would try to be Nana (as they called her) and then immediately they left the room she'd make some barbed comment. It sounded funny, and on some occasions I did laugh, but I knew how I would feel if I found out she was doing the same to me.

After only twenty-four hours inside the house we were forced to do live nominations. It was the thing I had dreaded happening. They warn you it's a possibility but I'd hoped to make my nominations in the privacy of the diary room. It's the most difficult part of the show and it's tricky finding reasons to give someone the boot. I thought about nominating Julie but decided to give her the benefit of the doubt. She might be good fun once she's dropped the pretence, I thought. In the end I went for Rhian. She hadn't done anything horrible but she was shy and I found it difficult to have a conversation with her. I think she found the whole experience overwhelming.

Then it was Julie's turn. And the woman who loved me, my clothes and every bit of telly I'd ever done, suddenly showed her true colours and stuck the knife in. 'I think Coleen's done her time,' she said. 'She's homesick and should therefore go home.' I could hardly believe it! Not once had I mentioned being homesick – I'd only been away for a couple of days. I realized then how much she wanted to win. But, unfortunately for her, she didn't get her way. Martin, Prince Lorenzo and Danica all nominated Jasmine and out she went.

Looking back, I believe Julie saw me as her biggest competition. In her mind, the other women were nobodies: she thought she could pick them off one at a time. It was important therefore to isolate me and make me appear unstable. Actually, she did quite a good job. All the time I was there I believed I was on my own in my mistrust of Julie. Everyone else appeared to love her. I was worried that, if my suspicions were wrong, I'd come across as such a bitch. Eventually, I went into the diary room and confessed everything. It was just what Big Brother wanted!

'Why don't you have it out with Julie?' they kept saying. Oh, yes, they'd have loved that – it would have made fantastic telly. But I was trying desperately to keep hold of my dignity and the last thing I wanted was to have a massive cat fight on national TV. I thought about Ray and Ciara sitting at home watching me. No chance, I thought.

Besides, what was I going to say? 'Please will you stop telling me that you love me'?

I was really lucky to have Cheryl in there with me. For some reason we made each other laugh hysterically. With my busy life there's no time for boredom, but in the *Big Brother* house there are hours and hours to fill and you need a friend in there to help you get through the monotony.

There's a great clip, which we all now call the shower scene. I must have watched it a thousand times since I came out. Cheryl couldn't attach her mic to the kaftan she always wore. She needed to slip it under her clothes so she'd climbed into the shower for a bit of privacy. After a few attempts she called me in to help but I wasn't any more use. I kept having to put my hand up her skirt and before long the two of us were giggling like schoolgirls while Lorenzo was standing outside trying to have a shave.

'Fuck me,' laughed Cheryl. 'I've got a Nolan on her knees trying to stick a microphone up my arse and a prince walking around in the bathroom!'

There were other times when Cheryl and I would

be sitting outside in the garden – me with my fag and her in her kaftan. Then Danica and Rhian would walk across the lawn, with their stunning bodies and beautiful clothes, and Cheryl and I would just look at one another and laugh at the absurdity of it all. It was, like, yeah, whatever! She was definitely my closest ally.

On day eight we were told we had to nominate two people to leave the house. Nominations truly are the most awful part of your time in there. It's really, really dreadful, and the longer you're in there, making friends and getting to know one another, the harder it is to do. Unsurprisingly this time around I chose Julie, and also Mike 'The Situation'. Mike was a lovely guy but he was a little strange in the house. I've since read that he has all sorts of problems, including mental-health worries, and I think that showed. Anyway, I had to nominate somebody and, apart from Julie, I really didn't have a good reason to want to lose anybody.

After we'd all been in the diary room, Big Brother gathered us in the living room to announce the results. 'The nominations for eviction are . . .' said Big Brother, pausing to build up dramatic tension, '. . . Julian, Prince Lorenzo, the Situation, Cheryl . . . and Coleen.' Gulp! As soon as I heard my name being read out my mind was racing. We all want to be liked – perhaps me especially, I'm terrible for needing that – and hearing that at least a couple of people wanted me out was like a stab to the heart. For the first few hours I kept looking at the others, trying to work out who had put the boot in. I didn't know it then, but it turned out to be Julie, Martin and Mike who had put my name forward. It was also gutting that Julie hadn't been nominated. Everybody else obviously loves her, I thought. How could I have been so wrong?

The next day I tried to forget about it and enjoy my last few hours in the house. I guessed that Cheryl and Julian would get enough votes to stay in so I told myself it could be me walking up the stairs the next evening.

On eviction night I chose my clothes carefully, put on a bit of makeup and tried to tease my hair into some sort of style. It was daft, really. I'd spent hours slobbing around in front of the cameras, but for eviction night it felt important to make an effort. It was live TV after all. We huddled together on the sofa and heard Brian Dowling's voice saying, 'You are now live on *Big Brother* . . . Do not swear!' We held each other's hands and waited nervously for the result.

Each time Brian read out a name the crowd would boo or cheer. Most of the housemates attracted a rousing 'Hooray,' which was great for them. But then Brian read out my name. Yes, there were definitely a few boos in there. I was mortified and convinced my time was up.

But I was wrong. Brian was saying, 'The second person to be evicted from the Big Brother House is . . . Cheryl!'

What? That couldn't be right. What on earth had happened? Until then it was a dead cert that Cheryl would win the entire thing. She hadn't done anything wrong and suddenly she was out. Ray told me afterwards that Cheryl didn't get much screen time and I think I know why. Before you go inside, the producers tell you not to sing because they would have to get clearance and pay copyright fees for anything that is aired. Well, Cheryl never stopped singing! It was probably difficult for them to find clips in which she wasn't! Her exit reminded me that we were at the mercy of the editors. The viewers saw only edited highlights and that was what the viewers were judging us on.

'I can't believe you're going,' I told her. 'I'm going to miss you so much.'

Cheryl was upset, too, but she took the result bravely and went out with a smile. 'See ya! Take care everybody!' she yelled. Then out she went.

Her departure rattled my confidence and once again made me question my feelings about Julie. Perhaps I was wrong. Perhaps she was a nice person, after all, and I was the bitch. I went into the diary room again that night and cried my eyes out. I wish now that I hadn't. It was hard for Ray to see me so distressed and not be able to do anything about it.

It sounds crazy, I know, but Julie just got to me in there. She made what could have been a wonderful experience into something quite nasty. I felt everybody in the house was her friend, especially Julian Clary, who was an angel and waited on her hand and foot. He never left her side. That woman didn't even get herself a glass of water. Julian helped her into bed, made her lunch and generally behaved like her twenty-four-hours-a-day carer. I worried that if people were so willing to be nice to her then I must have got her completely wrong.

One by one the housemates left. After Jasmine and Cheryl, Rhian, Samantha, Danica and Prince Lorenzo soon followed. That left Harvey, Ashley, Julian, Martin, Mike, Julie and me! From then on everything changed. Julie started following me around like a puppy, sharing her cigarettes and reminding me that 'us women' should stick together. She would give me what she called Nana kisses and try to win me over. But it was too late for any of that. By now I was desperate for her to go, so I smiled sweetly knowing I would nominate her the first chance I had.

The only time we had a clue at what was happening in the outside world was on eviction nights when the crowd continued to make known their thoughts on the remaining housemates.

One night I could hear them chanting, 'Get Julie out, get Julie out!' I can't tell you what that did for me. I wanted to run outside and hug every one of them. It was the first time I knew I wasn't going mad, that Julie Goodyear really was a class-A villain and that the people at home could see it.

But Julie wasn't ready to admit defeat. She turned to Julian and said, 'Don't worry, love. I'm sure they didn't mean it.'

Poor, gentle, kind Julian, who had only ever been an

absolute saint to her, was so hurt. 'Were they chanting "Get Julian out"?' he asked me, looking upset.

'God, no,' I reassured him. 'It was "Get Julie out." Don't listen to her!'

I don't know what I would have done in there without my three boys, Harvey, Ashley and Mike. They became like my children. It was like having three toddlers in the house who made me belly-laugh every single day. At other times they were so raucous I wanted to ground them and take their toys away. They were so naughty, but I loved them.

Then something happened to make the scales fall from their eyes where Julie was concerned. The boys were in the gym, along with Martin Kemp, and overheard her in the next-door bathroom ripping them apart, one by one. I could see from their faces that something had gone on, they were so upset. It was no surprise that when the nomination list was read that week, Julie's name was on it, alongside Martin's. I tried to keep a straight face but inside I was having a party. Oh, my God, was she fuming! She called us ageist and even shouted something too rude to be broadcast.

'I bet you feel great now nominating a seventy-year-old disabled pensioner,' she hissed. Hmm, I thought. Not many sweet old pensioners use that kind of language.

We'd all run out of cigarettes but she still had plenty and to get back at us she made it clear that she wouldn't be sharing. It's so boring in there that smoking is one of the only things that keeps you sane so Big Brother eventually let us have some more. Then the lighter went missing. Once more we needed Julie, but we knew we'd have to box clever.

'Julian, she loves you,' I said one night, when I hadn't had a cigarette for hours. 'Please be nice to her and ask her if you can borrow her lighter.'

So kind, gentle, loyal Julian asked her nicely. Do you know what she said? 'I wouldn't piss on any of you if you were on fucking fire.' Lovely.

On the night of the eviction, she dressed in a long sequinned cape and put on her 'Get it. Got it. Good' T-shirt and leopard-print tights, and sat waiting to hear her fate. *Please let it be Julie, please let it be Julie.* The voice in my head was so loud I felt sure she would hear it. Then Brian's voice was booming into the room.

'*Big Brother* house, this is Brian. Julie . . .' at this point the crowd outside gave a massive boo, '. . . Martin . . .' a huge cheer could be heard. 'For the last three days the great British public has been voting to save . . . I can now reveal that the celebrity with the least votes and who is the seventh to be evicted is . . .

'. . . Julie!'

My heart was doing somersaults. It was fabulous. To her credit, she took it well. She told us she loved us, then strolled out, her cape sparkling in the air behind her.

So she was gone. And then it hit me that I was the only woman left with five men. I was in the final! I was so thrilled that I needed to jump. I dashed into the bedroom and bounced up and down on my mattress.

Ciara told me later that she was cheering and jumping up and down with me on the sofa!

Those last few days were great. I got on so well with everyone who was left – even if they were male chauvinist pigs at heart.

Harvey said one day, 'Well, next to go will be Coleen.'

I was a bit put out. 'What makes you say that?' I asked.

'You know we all love you, Coleen, but it's women viewers who vote for the housemates and they'll keep the lads in, won't they?' he said, with a smile. And, hand on heart, I believed I would be the next to go. That was fine by me. I was happy to be the last woman standing. Plus, it would mean I was going home.

By now we all truly believed that Ashley would win. He was such a nice kid. So entertaining and funny and genuine and naïve that everybody simply loved him. But, on the night of the final, it wasn't my name they called. First up was Harvey, then Ashley, then Mike. We couldn't understand what was happening.

Julian, Martin and I were the last three. It was the weirdest feeling. I felt sure then that Martin would win, given that he had such a huge Spandau Ballet fan base. When we heard Brian announce his name as the next to go Julian and I could barely believe it.

Throughout our time in the house Julian had been quite understated and not at all how I'd expected him to be. He was sweet and friendly but he didn't show off that razor sharp sarcasm that you associate with his comedy act. Ray told me afterwards that Julian had been brilliantly funny in the diary room, which is presumably what eventually won it for him. It turned out that he'd had a master plan, after all, and good on him for doing so.

Those moments when you are made to wait before the winner is revealed seem to stretch on for ever. They do it on all the programmes now – *Dancing On Ice*, *The X Factor*, even *Strictly*. But it gives you time to chew over all manner of niggly thoughts. How had I come across to the viewers at home? Had the show been edited to make me look a complete bitch? How had Ray and the kids coped? Were they proud? Or embarrassed?

Julian and I sat together, holding hands, hardly daring to breathe. Come on, come on, I was thinking. Just say Julian's name and let me get back to my family!

'And the winner of *Celebrity Big Brother* 2012,' Brian was saying, 'is [long, long, long pause] Julian Clary!'

Julian was so surprised he immediately burst into tears and threw himself into my arms. I was so pleased for him and let him sob all over the shoulder of my smart black jacket.

'I've never won anything in my life,' he bawled. Later he would tell Brian Dowling, 'You've made a fifty-three-year-old homosexual very happy!'

But now I had to leave Julian and make my way to those *Big Brother* stairs and the door to the outside world. While you're in there, nobody wants to climb them because it means you've been evicted, but on the last day they looked like the best stairs ever!

The doors whooshed open, there was an immense roar from the crowd and the flash of cameras filled the darkness. It was so overwhelming I almost felt like turning round and running back inside. I'm not ready, I thought. I need another hour to have a cup of tea and prepare myself. But I had to go. The madness was happening all around me and I stepped nervously down the outside steps.

The first thing I saw was somebody holding up a massive poster saying, 'We're in the mood for Coleen.' Aw, that's nice, I thought. Then, standing next to the people with the poster, I saw Ray, Shane and Jake! I desperately wanted to feel their arms around me but I knew I had to do an interview with Brian first. I can't remember much of what was said – it was as if I was in a dream – but I do recall him asking about Julie and the crowd letting up a huge boo, which was heartening! 'She was a great housemate, she just didn't like me,' I managed to say. 'Even when she kissed me there was venom.'

As soon as the cameras cut for a commercial break, I ran over to my family. Ray threw his arms around me. 'You were spot on about Julie. You were the only one who got it,' he shouted, over the noise of the crowd. Oh, my God, I was so relieved!

I was taken to the studio where they film *Big Brother's Bit On the Side*. They needed to do the big exit interview, during which I was shown all the nasty gibes that Julie had made about me. If they'd been clever they'd have shown them to me while we were both still inside the house. My God, then they would have had the fireworks they were looking for. But now Julie herself was sitting next to me in the studio and I wasn't going to give the producers what they wanted. Just stay professional, I told myself. Smile and keep your cool.

After the cameras had stopped rolling, Julie turned to me and grabbed my hand. 'I just want you to know that I loved you from the moment you walked in and I love you today,' she said. 'Don't listen to all that. It just breeds paranoia.'

I'm not listening to anyone else. I'm listening to you slagging me off! I thought. 'You know what, Julie?' I said. 'You are completely insane.' Then I stood up and walked away. I've never seen her since.

But none of that mattered now. I was out and back with Ray and the boys, which was all I cared about. Ciara was too young to be allowed on to the *Big Brother* set so I had to wait a bit longer to see her. But my family was very nearly complete once again.

'God, I've missed you,' Ray told me that night, stroking my hair. 'I think it was not being able to call you that got to me the most. I kept going to dial your number and then I'd remember that I'd go straight to voicemail.'

Being away from Ray had made me realize, too, that he is really the only person I want to speak to most of the time. It made me thank my lucky stars that we'd been able to get through our difficulties and come out the other side stronger than ever. I promised myself it would be a very long time indeed before I left his side again.

We went back to the hotel and partied with the rest of the housemates and their friends and families until gone five in the morning. Julie was a no-show but I certainly didn't miss her. It was a great way to finish the experience off.

Exhausted, I crawled into bed at six. Just forty-five minutes later I was being woken up by a knock on the hotel-room door. It was the girl who had been booked to do my hair and makeup. I had to do a shoot later that day for *OK!* magazine and Neil, bless him, knew that after three and a half weeks inside the house my roots would need retouching. He was right. I looked like a skunk!

The producers had returned my phone but, strangely, it took me twenty-four hours to switch it back on. I hadn't missed one single aspect of it. I wasn't ready to go back into the real world just yet. I didn't want to read any of the vile things people might have written about me during my time in the house. As it turned out, there hadn't been too much negative publicity, thank God!

One of the first voices I wanted to hear was Bernie's. I needed to know how she was coping and if she'd had any new test results. Every night inside the house Bernie had been on my mind. We were still at the stage of keeping her second diagnosis a secret and it was difficult not being able to talk about her. I knew that if her condition had worsened the family would have been able to get a message through to me, but I'd hated not swapping texts with her.

So there had been times when I'd yearned for Bernie and the rest of my family and, of course, there were the run-ins with Julie but, believe it or not, I still miss the house. It was like being on holiday with great mates – apart from you-know-who. I miss the peace and the fact that nobody could get to me. I wasn't expected to do anything or be anyone or go anywhere. It was brilliant.

And it taught me quite a lot about myself, too. I learned that I care desperately what people think of me. That was a bit of a surprise, I must admit. We all like to be liked, but I was struck by how much the boos and the cheers affected my confidence. Hearing the boos the first time I was nominated made me feel physically sick. Reaching the final was a real boost, and when those doors opened and the crowd gave me a warm reception, it was as good as being named the winner.

So, would I do it again? Absolutely. I'm glad I did it. Despite the tears and the tantrums, it really was a most amazing and bizarre experience.

# Chapter Eight

'So, tell me, are you going to do a Sinatra and end up doing fifteen farewell tours?' asked the gorgeous Alan Titchmarsh, when the girls and I appeared on his show that October. Linda, Maureen and I looked at each other. 'No way! Our hips won't hold out any longer. This is it!' And we meant it. The Nolans were never, ever, ever going to tour together again – except for this one last time . . .

I'd gone into *Celebrity Big Brother* to buy myself some time off. Now, two months on, I was loving the break. With no *Loose Women* or *This Morning* I would potter around our house in Wilmslow simply being Ciara's mum and Ray's wife. I'd get up early to do the school run, spend time with friends, watch daytime telly and be there in the afternoon to take Ciara to the stables, then cook her tea. She'd gone back to secondary school knowing I was at home and not two hundred miles away in a hotel or a television studio – and that meant a lot to both of us. There was a very special project on the horizon though that was exciting enough to lure me away from my cosy family life.

Six months earlier I had been pushing a trolley around Waitrose when opportunity suddenly came knocking. I was in the biscuit aisle, deciding between chocolate digestives and some Hobnobs when my phone rang. It was Neil.

'Now, hear me out before you say no,' he laughed.

'Oh god, what now, do I even dare to ask?' I replied.

'Well, we've had an offer for you and the girls to do one final tour. What do you reckon? Could be amazing to go out with a bang!'

I stepped away from the Hobnobs. So many thoughts and emotions were rushing through my brain that I couldn't answer. Did I want to go back on the road? Would another tour spark off a new round of battles with Anne and Denise? What would Ray and Ciara say? Would anyone want to come and – most importantly – could we still pull it off? The I'm In The Mood Again tour had been so wonderful I didn't want to tarnish the memory. Back in 2009 we'd ended on a high. None of us had ever dreamed it would go so well but we'd had complete sell-outs every night. We'd had huge sets, big budgets and performed at the UK's biggest arenas – was it really possible we could do it again?

Neil was still on the phone. 'It's going to be a bit different this time round,' he was chattering on. 'We'll make it more intimate and use loads of footage from over the years, really tell the Nolan story. It's a chance to say thank you and goodbye to the fans and would be a proper, fitting end to everything, to really go out on a high.'

'Let's ask the girls,' I said. 'But if they're in, so am I.'

Linda and Maureen felt exactly the same as I did. 'Christ, yes!' was Linda's immediate response.

Maureen, ever the sensible one, simply said, 'That would be great!'

When it was suggested to Bernie she couldn't have been more excited. 'Absolutely, it's exactly what we should do,' she said.

Ray and the kids were up for it, too. They'd all been involved with the 2009 tour and they knew how much it had meant to me. They started counting the days before we could do it all over again.

It was decided that this time we'd approach things very differently. There wasn't the budget to do a repeat of 2009 so it had to be something fresh – we didn't want people to come with the same expectations and be disappointed. The promoters suggested we choose smaller, more intimate venues. There would still be the same high-quality production but on a more manageable scale. Plus, this time we would do a sort of personal review of our entire career. The film footage of our lives would appear on the screen behind us. From black-and-white pictures of us as child performers, to the terrible 1970s outfits on *Top of the Pops*, to bubble perms and eighties fashions.

The music for the I'm In The Mood Again tour had been chosen to reflect how we'd all survived our various struggles in life, such as divorce, illness and widowhood. We'd covered the big diva songs such as 'It's Raining Men', 'I Need A Hero' and, of course, 'I Will Survive', and the fans had loved it. But they'd also been a bit miffed we hadn't done more of our own hits. This time round, we decided, we'd give them what they wanted and do all of them in full. Out would come 'Don't Make Waves', 'Gotta Pull Myself Together', 'Who's Gonna Rock You' and 'Attention To Me'.

We chose our favourite theatres, places we'd known and loved before. The tour would kick off on 15 February at the Nottingham Royal Centre and take in the Manchester Apollo, the Blackpool Opera House and the Plymouth Pavilions. It would finish four weeks later at the Liverpool Echo Arena and include – much to our delight – Wembley. Even at the height of our success we never did Wembley. I felt sick with nerves and excitement all at the same time.

But a few months later, in the autumn of 2012, the biggest question in my mind centred around Bernie. Was she well enough to get through the gruelling schedule of a nationwide tour? She was the star of the show, our fantastic lead vocalist. She was the first up on stage and the last to take her bow. I knew that, if she could, she would love the chance to do it all again. She was determined not to let the cancer take the opportunity away from her, though, and I tried not to let the words of the Venice Beach fortune-teller creep into my head.

I thought about how much Bernie loved perform-ing and how she'd sparkled and shone during the 2009 tour. Singing was Bernie's life: it was all she'd ever wanted to do. If this was a chance for her to spar-kle again, I didn't want to be the one to take it away from her.

Her schedule was ridiculous at the time we had been planning the tour, though. She was already touring all over the country in her role as Mama Morton in *Chicago*, and after that she had a panto planned. The Nolans' Farewell Tour had had to be slotted in afterwards in February 2013.

I tried to imagine how it would feel that last March night in Liverpool, knowing we would never perform together again. With every business meeting we had I realized it was exactly the right thing to do. Sod it, I thought, life was too short to worry about what-ifs. I could see that every show would be tinged with sadness, knowing that it was one performance closer to our last, but I was desperate to get going.

By September 2012, Bernie had told her daughter that the cancer had spread. When it had first returned, she was determined to protect Erin from the whole truth. She felt it was enough that she and Steve had to live with the knowledge and didn't want Erin to worry. But then the doctors discovered the cancer had disappeared from her brain and Bernie was ecstatic. She wanted to share her good news with her daughter and now she could tell her, honestly, that the tablets were working. It gave her a terrific boost.

She still hadn't gone public, though. And even as we were having meetings to plan the new tour, she was enduring the side effects of the strong drugs she was taking. The pills gave her mouth ulcers and made the skin on the soles of her feet peel. My heart broke for my brave sister – but she wasn't having any of it.

'Look, Bernie,' I said to her one day when the girls came round to my house to put the final touches to the play list. 'Don't feel you need to push yourself so much. Let us support you more.'

Every time she winced because of the mouth ulcers, or slipped her shoes off because of her blistered feet, I could almost feel the pain myself. The others were the same. We would have done anything to relieve her of it if we could.

'Yes, I can do this bit in the song. You can have a rest on a stool!' Linda joked. But Bernie wouldn't hear of it.

'Don't feel sorry for me,' she'd scold. 'I've got to keep on living and working. I'm not going to sit back and let it get me.'

In September we were in the studios having our publicity shots taken. The tour was to be sponsored by Marisota, the fashion brand that I design a range for, and the company had arranged for us to wear these very glamorous gold sequinned jackets from my line. As I stood next to the other three girls, our hair and makeup perfect and our jackets shimmering under the bright lights, I allowed myself a degree of hope.

'God, you're amazing, Bernie,' I said. 'You're looking really well.'

She smiled and, typical of her, shrugged off the compliment. 'My bloody feet are killing me, though!' she laughed. 'Can we get these pictures done so I can take my shoes off?'

It was a lovely day. The girls from Marisota, whom I adore, were there and, with Bernie in such great form, it was an amazing shoot. The photographs from that day are among my favourite Nolans pictures ever. I've had one framed and it sits, pride of place, on my mantelpiece. In it Linda and I are on each end of the line-up and, in the centre, there's Bernie and Maureen. Bernie's fingernails are painted red and her blonde hair is shining with health. It looks to me like all three sisters are holding on to her to keep her with us for ever. I think we probably were.

On 25 September we announced news of the tour and the response could not have been better. The Nolans seemed to be on every TV screen and in every newspaper. 'NOLAN SISTERS CONFIRM THEIR FAREWELL BRITISH TOUR,' screamed the headlines. We were being whisked from one TV studio to the next to talk about the shows and, despite her bravery, I could see that Bernie was fighting the illness daily. Yes, she was pulling off brilliant performances every night in *Chicago*, but I think us girls could see how much the effort was costing her. Sometimes she would be in agony and she'd have to ask the wardrobe mistress to fit special pads in her shoes so her feet didn't hurt. Other times she couldn't face the pain of eating because of the ulcers in her mouth. It seemed hardly credible that when the Nolans' tour kicked off she would be well enough to perform, but we never gave up hope. If she had ever turned round and said to us, 'I'm sorry, girls, but I don't think I can carry on,' we'd have cancelled in a flash. But she never did, and we didn't want to pass on any negative thoughts. This was Bernie, after all, and quite honestly you wouldn't bet good money against her.

On 28 September, the day the tickets went on sale, the four of us were due to do an interview on *BBC Breakfast* but during the night disaster struck. Bernie was in Sheffield with *Chicago* and had planned to travel to the BBC's Salford studios early the next morning for the news programme. As usual, she'd soldiered on as Mama Morton, but by the end of the show she was exhausted and feeling unwell.

She sounded really fed up. 'Oh, God, I'm so sorry, Col,' she said. 'I hate letting you all down but I just can't drive myself over to Manchester. I can barely get myself back to the hotel.'

'Don't even think about it,' I told her, meaning it. 'Just have some rest and concentrate on getting better.'

But what were we going to tell the BBC? There is a darker side of our business in that sometimes you have to put personal worries aside and carry on with a smile on your face, whatever's happening in real life. I knew Bernie had sworn us to secrecy over the fact that she was unwell and wanted us to promote the tour.

'I know it's really, really difficult, but we're just going to have to find a way to do it without her,' Neil told us. He was clearly concerned but determined to be positive. 'I've spoken to her and it's what she wants you to do. Hopefully, she'll be back with us for the next one.' I could hear in Neil's voice that he feared we'd turned a dark corner too, but for the sake of Bernie we all had to carry on.

Ray supporting
Rick Astley on tour.

Ray was thrilled to be
playing in huge arenas
like this one.

I was over the moon for
Ray but we had no idea
what a strain his job would
put on our marriage.

A childhood dream come true: my beautiful horse, Orla.

Ciara winning the first of many rosettes with her pride and joy: Paddy the pony!

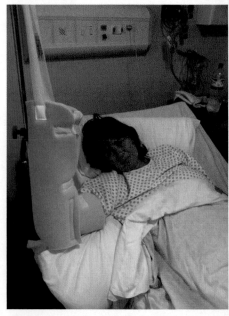

I almost lost my fingers during a freak accident in the stables. My eyes still water at the memory of the pain!

I was so excited going into the *Celebrity Big Brother* house – but terrified too! Here I am on launch night (*left*) and leaving the house as runner-up (*right*).

*From left*: Julie Goodyear, Ashley McKenzie and I inside the house. Julie and I didn't exactly see eye-to-eye . . . I think my expression says it all!

In 2012 I starred as the Fairy Godmother in *Cinderella* at the Liverpool Empire Theatre.

Atomic Kitten star Liz McClarnon played Cinderella in the show and we became great friends.

Actually, Ray tried to persuade me to stand in front of the taxi advert but this was as close as I would go!

This dress was so hard to walk in. It's not easy being a fairy!

*From left:* our dear friends Nick and Paul, myself, Ciara and Ray, and another good friend, Laura.

Welcome to Hollywood!

Coleen meets Coleen! We bumped into Coleen and Wayne Rooney at our hotel in LA.

On Venice Beach. Our day out took a dark turn after meeting a fortune-teller.

Backstage on tour with Ciara.

What a scary pair! Ray and I all dressed up and ready to go to my charity Halloween ball.

Ready to party. Doesn't Ciara look like a little angel?

Ciara and I have a great mother-daughter relationship.

Ray and I have learnt to make time for one another and we're now back on track.

A rare holiday – this time at the Trevi Fountain in Rome.

This was the last photo I took of Bernie. Here she is at her husband Steve's fiftieth birthday.

The last few years taught me that, above all, family comes first.

I felt torn in two. I hated going on TV and not telling the truth but Neil was right. It was important to Bernie that we all carried on as normal and she wasn't ready to share her news with the public. She wanted people to go and see her in *Chicago*, she wanted people to come and see the tour. Like he said, we had no choice. We had to sit on the breakfast TV sofa and drum up some excitement for the nine a.m. release of concert tickets.

Linda, Maureen and I travelled to Salford, each getting up at five to reach the studios on time. As we sat in Hair and Makeup the three of us exchanged nervous glances, knowing we had to stick to our story.

'Oh, God, I feel sick,' said Linda, after we nominated her to tell the fib. 'I'm bound to fluff my lines and blush. I'm not a good liar.'

'Just do your best, Linda,' Maureen urged. 'Bernie would want you to.'

Sitting on the famous red sofas, we waited as they ran the usual video of 'I'm In The Mood For Dancing', with Bernie looking young and healthy and singing brilliantly. Then the film finished and the presenter Charlie Stayt was introducing us.

'Welcome all, but solve a mystery for us,' he said. 'There's someone missing. What's happened?'

Then Linda showed us what an amazing actress she really is. Smiling sweetly for the cameras, she said, 'Oh, Bernie's in Sheffield doing *Chicago* and she decided to drive herself up this morning. Trouble is, the car's come to a shuddering halt.'

I heard myself saying quickly, 'I told her to have it serviced but, oh, no, she wouldn't listen!' I'm always like that when I try to tell a fib, I start gabbling. Inside my brain I was going, Shut up! Shut up!

But by now Linda had really hit her stride. 'But don't worry, Bernie will be doing *Chicago* tonight in Sheffield, and she'll definitely be on the tour with us.' She smiled. After that Charlie and his co-anchor Louise Minchin moved on and let us chatter about the upcoming concerts. By the time our slot was over my nerves were frayed. I'm never doing anything like that again, I thought.

But I was going to have to. Five days later we were booked for *The Alan Titchmarsh Show* at the ITV studios on London's South Bank – the same studios where we recorded *Loose Women* so for me it was like going home. But I was troubled about Bernie. All three of us doubted she would be well enough to make an appearance – and we were right. The day before the interview she was admitted to hospital near her home in Weybridge, suffering from cellulitis. It's a skin infection that causes inflammation and is really quite dangerous. It's not supposed to be linked to breast cancer but, oddly, Linda had had it when she was having her own treatment. I think it must be something to do with the body being vulnerable because of the treatment. Whatever the cause was, Bernie didn't look or feel well enough to be on television.

*I'm so pissed off*, she texted. *It's driving me mad missing all this stuff – I should be with you.*

I called Neil. 'Should we really be keeping this going?' I asked. 'There's no way she's going to be well enough to do the tour. Perhaps we should just pull it now.'

But Neil's such a great agent and he always knows what to do. 'I know it's so hard for you to know what's really wrong,' he replied, 'but just tell the truth about the cellulitis. She's insistent that she wants you to say she's going to be on the tour, which, of course, is what we all want. I feel exactly the same as you and if it were my call we would pull it now, but what she wants is to carry on, so we'll just have to keep going until she says otherwise. She needs something to aim for, so just do your best for her.'

With a familiar feeling of dread, Linda, Maureen and I headed for London. We'd been booked to sing on the show but without Bernie we couldn't do it just-ice. I don't think any of us was in the mood for dancing. Instead the three of us sat nervously on Alan's sofa, laughing and joking about failing hips while trying to explain Bernie's absence.

'Unfortunately Bernie has cellulitis,' said Linda, once again taking on the responsibility for us all. 'It came up all of a sudden in the middle of the night.'

Alan was great and wished Bernie a speedy recovery. I managed to raise a laugh with a joke about our age. 'We're not worried about our hips or knees, we can get those pinned,' I said. 'It's our faces I'm worried about!'

To my relief, he also changed the subject by asking me about the veteran DJ Jimmy Savile. His years of molesting young girls had just been in the headlines and I'd taken part in a documentary about the whole disgusting episode. In the programme, I'd revealed how Savile had hugged me inappropriately when I'd appeared with him on *Top of the Pops*. It was 1979, when I was only fourteen, and the girls were performing on the show. There's a video on YouTube of me standing next to him as he introduces the Nolans. I've got a pudding-bowl haircut and I'm wearing a lavender-coloured dress and jacket. I look no older than Ciara is now but, despite this, Savile's arm is around my waist and he's pulling me towards him. It makes me shudder to look at it.

Worse than that, though, was that after the cameras were off us he invited me back to his hotel suite. He asked me where I lived and I told him Blackpool. 'I'm going to be doing a show there soon and I've got a suite at the Imperial Hotel,' he said. 'When I'm there you must come down and see me. You can see the suite.'

The Imperial was Blackpool's poshest hotel and I remember being quite excited and telling my sisters. Far from being impressed, they were appalled. 'That's not right, Coleen,' they said. 'That's just weird.' They probably saved me from his clutches. Why else would a fully grown man ask a fourteen-year-old girl to go to his hotel room? But, saying that, I would never describe myself as one of his victims. What he did to me was merely uncomfortable. It was nothing compared to the real victims' situations. When the truth finally came out, I was sorry that Savile wasn't still alive to answer the charges – but it was a good thing that those he had abused could finally be heard.

'Who knows what would have happened if it hadn't have been for your sisters?' Alan said.

'God, yeah, Jimmy Savile had no chance up against the witches of Eastwick!' I joked. Perhaps we shouldn't have been laughing about such a horrible topic but, to be honest, it was a relief to steer the conversation away from the missing Bernie and our tour.

Afterwards we sat in the green room, thinking about what we should do next. We all felt such great love towards the fans who were paying good money to see us in February. It was touching to know that they were still supporting us after all the years. If we cancelled, they would get their money back but, still, we hated to let them down.

Then there was the psychological effect that cancelling would have on Bernie. She would be devastated. Not being able to perform one last time with her sisters would be like a reality check for her – that she really wasn't well enough to do it. Accepting her condition was the hardest battle of all and we worried it would set her back to a place where she couldn't fight any longer. It was a dreadful dilemma and we were torn between Bernie, our duty to our fans and the thought that we didn't want people getting excited and paying money for concerts that were never going to happen.

For three more weeks, even though he had informed the tour company about Bernie's health and they were happy to continue, Neil held off signing the final insurance document that would definitely commit us to doing the shows. The contract said that, should one of us fall too ill to perform, the remaining three would have to continue. If we refused the company could lose a lot of money and that weighed heavily on all of us as we would never want to cause anyone any problems. I'm so glad that Neil made us aware of what signing the document would mean – lots of agents just tell you to sign on the dotted line and you do – that's how we lost so much money over the years as the Nolans – but not Neil. He's as honest as the day and has always pointed out the bad as well as the good in everything.

'I don't know about you but if Bernie's sick in hospital the last thing I'll be doing is singing and dancing at a theatre in Nottingham,' said Maureen. 'I'll be at her bedside, holding her hand.'

'God, yeah,' I said. 'If I get a phone call saying she's ill I'm not going on any stage. I'll be with my sister. Don't mention this to Bernie, though. You know what she's like. She'll have us signing that contract before you can say, "Knife."'

We all agreed. It was the most difficult decision ever but, in the end, practicalities won the day. We simply couldn't sign that insurance document.

'You're going to have to be the one to tell Bernie, though,' I said to Neil, once the decision was made. 'She'll only take it fom you. And I'm not sure you can tell her the truth. It would destroy her.'

True to his word, he spoke to her and told her it

was off. I'm still not sure what he said – something about ticket sales being disappointing, or some legal wrangle with the insurance, perhaps, but he let her down as gently as he could. Bernie, as we suspected, was heartbroken and, as usual, remained upbeat – 'I'm sure we'll do it again when everything gets sorted,' she said soon after. I smiled and nodded, but knew that she would have been even more upset if she had known the truth – the tour would never happen.

It was decided that the announcement would be made on 29 October. By now we were all pleased to drop the pretence, and to some extent Bernie must have felt it, too. She decided she would take control of what was happening and do a newspaper interview the day before. She could tell her story her own way and pass the message on to other women in her situation that all was not lost. That was really important to her.

Her producer on *Chicago* had been amazingly understanding and supportive, and had allowed her a few days off so that she could be at home with Erin when the newspaper interview was published. The Saturday night before it came out, Bernie emailed relatives and friends and each member of the show's cast and crew because she wanted to break the news to them herself. Family members back in Ireland had no idea that she was so ill and she couldn't let them see it first in the newspaper. It was typical of Bernie, thinking of others when anybody else would, understandably, have been thinking of themselves.

I was at home with Ray and I knew Bernie planned to send her email. I imagined her sitting at home in Weybridge, tapping away on her computer. I could picture her hitting the send button and her dreadful message winging its way across the ether to all those poor people. They were about to receive such terrible news.

'God, Ray, what would it be like to find that in your inbox?' I said. 'There's no good way to do these things but it's going to be such a shock for everyone – especially the *Chicago* lot who've been working with her every night.'

'Christ, yeah,' he said, reaching over to place my hand in his. 'But you know Bernie, it's important she does this her way.'

The next morning I got out of bed early and went downstairs to find the *Sunday Mirror* on the doormat in the porch. And there it was: 'BERNIE NOLAN – MY CANCER HAS RETURNED AND IS INCURABLE'. I'd been carrying the knowledge since April but seeing the words splashed across the newspaper like that was shattering. My heart broke for my sister, my niece and my brother-in-law. It made me want to gather up my own family and hold them tight.

Bernie was quoted, saying, 'OK, it's not curable. But the doctors have promised me the cancer is treatable – it's containable. I refuse to sit around like I've got a death sentence hanging over my head. I'm going to fight this for ever. It can get stuffed.'

I knew it must be a relief for her to share her secret

at last. Bernie was such an honest person – she hated lying. It was hard for the rest of the family to keep her struggle private so it must have been terrible for her.

'For friends who don't know and are reading this, I know it's awful to hear,' she said. 'But I hope they understand why I haven't been able to tell them yet.

'I just couldn't face ringing everyone. What do you say? "Hi, how are you? Well, I've got incurable cancer, have you got any news?"'

The last straw, she said, had been appearing on TV with Lorraine Kelly during Breast Cancer Awareness Week and not being able to be completely truthful about her condition.

'When she asked me how I was I just changed the subject, but that's the sort of thing that doesn't sit well with me,' she told the newspaper. 'And who can say what that sort of stress does to your health, wondering who knows, who doesn't know? I apologize to Lorraine now but I couldn't have said it then.

'My daughter didn't know the full story so I couldn't say, "Actually, funny you should ask, because it's back, and it's spread." Erin might have been watching. I did hate lying like that.'

She was searingly honest. She described how angry Steve was, because only months before the doctors had been confident the cancer was gone. In fact, we were all angry. None of us could understand what had happened. There's a massive part of me that still wants an explanation from those doctors. Bernie went from being in full remission to suddenly having it back again worse than ever. What were they missing? How could they have been so wrong?

But Bernie was stronger than all of us. She wanted to put out a positive message to other women with breast cancer. She'd had such a magnificent response from women all over the country that she couldn't bear to be anything other than inspirational. Plus, she was convinced that part of the reason the cancer had disappeared from her brain was to do with her optimism.

'I wake up in the morning bright, happy, and then it hits me. I've got incurable cancer,' she told the paper. 'But then I think, Oh, well, feck it. Get up and get on with it.'

The following morning the announcement about the tour was made. The promoter, Kennedy Street, put out a statement, 'Due to very unforeseen circumstances, the Nolans' farewell tour has had to be cancelled.' It was very sad, but our responsibility was to Bernie.

Next we put up an announcement on the Nolans' website: 'Dear Fans, we are SO sorry that our tour is postponed but we promise we'll be back on the road to see you all again soon. Until then, all our love, Coleen, Bernie, Linda and Maureen.'

Bernie's *Chicago* tour was due to finish in Plymouth on 1 December but by now she was struggling. She'd developed a really stubborn cough and her immune system was so low that she couldn't shake it off. Every night she would turn up, determined to go on stage, and every night she would cough so much that her voice couldn't make it. I knew she was heartbroken not to be able to go out with a flourish. Nevertheless, she stayed with the company regardless, celebrating the end of the run with her friends.

I often wonder what I would have done in her situation. I can't help thinking I'd have spent those months at home with my family, grabbing as much time with them as I could. That's not to say that Bernie didn't want that, too – she just had a stronger drive to perform. She'd say that working distracted her and stopped the darker thoughts of what lay ahead. And, of course, she was trying to earn as much money as she could while she was able to. As a mum I could understand that burning desire to look after her family: it's what you do. There aren't enough words for me to express how proud of her I was.

With the tour now off, I had one more job to focus on. I'd been asked to take part in *Cinderella* at the Liverpool Empire. The timing was difficult, as I didn't feel much like getting stuck into such a happy production, plus it had been twenty-one years since I'd last been in panto. What am I doing? I asked myself. But Ciara was excited to see her mum as the Fairy Godmother and *Cinderella* has always been a favourite – it reminded me of being a kid at Christmas time in Blackpool. I was following in fitting footsteps, too. In 2009 Bernie had played the Fairy Godmother in *Cinderella* at the Manchester Opera House. And in 2011 Linda had played the bad fairy opposite Maureen who played the good fairy – no typecasting there, then! – in *Jack and the Beanstalk* at London's Shaw Theatre in Euston. It was time for me to slap on the greasepaint and get involved.

As soon as I arrived in Liverpool for rehearsals I knew I'd made the right decision. It was going to be a top-notch production with fabulous costumes and magical special effects. At one stage I waved my wand and Cinders and her six mice were transformed into Princess Crystal and her brilliant white Shetland ponies!

I was also working with some great people. Two famous Liverpool personalities, Pete Price and Pauline Daniels, were playing the Ugly Sisters, and ex-Atomic Kitten, Liz McClarnon, was to be Cinderella. We had such a laugh. They had to literally pour me into my huge confection of a dress. I looked like something out of *My Big Fat Gypsy Wedding*! What with the horses and the lovely audiences, I felt right at home. I even got to sing 'I'm In The Mood For Dancing'. I can't get away from that song!

*Cinderella* ran from 14 December until 6 January and, by the end of it, I was exhausted. Doing so many shows a week had taken it out of me and, though the panto had made Christmas that year really special, I was glad when the final curtain fell.

But if going into panto was tough for me, God knew how Bernie would do it. Nevertheless, with *Chicago* finished, she went straight into rehearsing *Sleeping Beauty* at the Devonshire Park Theatre in East-bourne, playing the Wicked Fairy. Her stamina was incredible – I don't think she had so much as a day off between the end of *Chicago* and the start of the panto rehearsals. Her cough was still plaguing her, though, and she'd been forced to pre-record her songs, which she hated doing.

During the opening week she was a complete trouper and did everything in her power to make the show go on. With both of us being such busy working mums we didn't get to see each other as much as we'd have liked but we'd text almost every day. Suddenly her texts stopped sounding jokey and defiant and started to terrify me. *Feeling crap today*, she'd say. *Can't eat – have even stopped drinking wine!*

Linda was desperately worried, too. 'Oh, my God, Col. I spoke to Bernie last night and she told me that she's throwing up every night after the show. That's not good. Somebody needs to make her pull out and go back home to Steve and Erin,' she said.

We all agreed with Linda. But Bernie wouldn't give in. Then, on 21 December, she received the devastating results of her latest scans and some of her famous fight began to desert her. The cancer was back in her brain and was now making its evil way through her bones and liver. The oral chemo that she'd been taking was no longer doing its job, and she was told she'd have to go back on to intravenous drugs. Poor, poor Bernie.

She phoned to tell me the news. 'I'm just letting everyone know what the doctors are saying now,' she said, her bright and breezy voice sounding almost convincing. 'But it could be worse. They could be stopping the treatment completely. They obviously think the chemo is worth a try.'

'Well, yes, of course it is,' I said. 'You've got to take everything they throw at you.' Her news was so awful but I knew I couldn't cry. That would come later, out of earshot of Bernie. She had taught me well.

She worked right up until Christmas, then had a few days off with the family. Maureen, Ritchie and Linda went down to Weybridge to stay with them, too. Steve transformed the house into a Christmas grotto, with snow sprayed on the windows and a beautifully decorated tree. We always speak to each other on Christmas Day, and when I called later that evening, they were all curled up in front of the fire watching *It's A Wonderful Life*. Bernie's once powerful voice was no more than a whisper, though.

'If she tries talking properly she has a coughing fit,' Maureen told me. 'We're trying to convince her not to go back to work tomorrow. What's going to happen if she does that on stage?'

On Boxing Day Bernie called in sick. I know how much that would have upset her. For Bernie the show really did have to go on. She did the same for the next few days until eventually she had to face the truth. She would not be going back. Finally, after keeping it from him, she admitted how ill she was now feeling to Neil, who was her manager too. 'Bernie, your health is more important than any work commitment,' he told her. 'I'll get you out of the panto today.' Neil later told me he was relieved because he had been trying to persuade her to give it up for months knowing that it was the wrong decision for her to do it, but Bernie had insisted on carrying on. She refused to believe she didn't have long.

The cruellest blow of all was the way the cancer was stealing her voice. Hearing her whisper on the telephone gave me an awful jolt.

'Has she been like that all the time you've been there?' I asked Maureen.

'It's so upsetting, Col,' she told me. 'Linda and I can't see her getting her voice back. This will be the thing that crushes her.'

More than any of us, Bernie lived for singing. She kept asking the doctors if her vocal cords would recover, and for a long time they refused to give a proper answer. It made her extremely angry. If she was willing to face the truth, her doctors needed to be honest with her, she said.

After weeks of pushing she was finally referred to a specialist, who put a camera down her throat to see what was going on. The doctors had told her that she had vocal paralysis, which had been caused by tumours pressing on her left vocal cord. Surgery was an option, but it was a difficult and dangerous procedure – one that might even kill her. Even with Bernie's great love of singing, she decided it was not a risk she wanted to take. When she was offered speech therapy she grabbed at it. She was willing to give almost anything a try.

When Linda phoned to tell me the specialist's verdict, I knew we were approaching the end. 'She's never going to sing again, Col,' she said. 'I could cry for her. But, of course, she won't let me.'

Something would have died in Bernie that day. If they'd told her she'd never walk again or that her eyesight would go, she'd have been able to accept that. But losing her voice was the final blow.

'I don't know what to say, Linda,' I told her. 'It's like the bastard cancer has won.'

Bernie had always been a great one for setting herself goals. When she was first told that she was going to die, she simply said, 'No, I can't. I'm going to be here for Erin's fourteenth birthday.' Then the next goal was her wedding anniversary. It seemed to me that after she lost the ability to sing there were no more goals left.

Not long after that Linda phoned again to say she'd seen Bernie and was worried. 'She's started slurring her words,' she told me. 'And she's finding it hard to see properly. Poor Bernie, it's just crap for her.'

The words of the fortune-teller on Venice Beach came back to torment me once again. As I lay in bed that night, alongside Ray, I couldn't stop myself voicing my darkest fears. 'Bernie won't survive this, you know,' I whispered. I'd hoped he would argue and tell me that I was wrong, but he didn't. Instead he put his arms around me and we both cried. I could feel his body rising and falling in pain. Neither of us could find words to comfort the other.

And then, bloody hell, the next day she bounced right back! My phone pinged and I could see it was a text from Bernie, telling me of her plans for 2013.

*I've decided I'm taking Erin and Steve to Venice – I want to show Erin where her dad asked me to marry him*, she said. *Then I want to go to Spain and then take a road trip around England to see all the beautiful places I've never been to. After that we're going to spend summer in New York and next Christmas in a chalet in the Alps!* It was as if she was frantically trying to stuff her remaining time with happiness.

*But first, let's all meet up in Blackpool at February half-term to celebrate Linda and Steve's birthdays. I want to have a party!* I almost laughed in disbelief.

I showed Ray the message. 'She's not going to be well enough, is she? What shall I say?' I asked him.

'Bloody hell, just tell her yes!' he said. So I did. If Bernie was sticking two fingers up at the cancer then so was I.

*Absolutely*, I told her. *Can't wait, see you in Feb!'*

It's shocking now to think that the Nolans' farewell tour had been scheduled to start that month. On 15 February Bernie, Linda, Maureen and I should have been standing in the wings of the stage at the Nottingham Royal Centre, our hearts thumping with the anticipation of performing live.

We couldn't have guessed that instead we would be together for a very different reason – to say our good-byes to our beloved Bernie.

# Chapter Nine

The Bernie sitting in the restaurant in Blackpool was a very different Bernie from the one I'd seen several months before. Everyone was gathering at a lovely place called Sapori to celebrate Linda's birthday and I'd driven over from Wilmslow for the occasion. Earlier that day, Linda had phoned to say she didn't think Bernie was going to be well enough to attend.

'You know how she hates to miss a party,' I laughed. 'I bet I'll walk in and she'll be sitting at the head of the table.'

I was right, but when I saw her I was shocked. Perhaps the others had seen Bernie more recently and hadn't noticed the change in her so much, but to me the deterioration was worrying. The last time I'd seen her she'd had more hair. Now she looked thin, tired and fragile. The meal lasted two and a half hours and she coughed non-stop. Every time she lifted a fork to her mouth she'd have another coughing fit.

'God, Bernie, are you all right?' I asked her.

'Oh, I'm fine, but this coughing is driving me bloody mad!' she answered.

By ten thirty p.m. poor Bernie was almost asleep on Steve's shoulder so he took her back to my brother Brian's house, where they were staying. I drove back to

Cheshire that Saturday night, thinking how poorly she looked. When I got home I went into Ciara's bedroom to spend a few moments watching her sleep. With her arms flung behind her and her hair spread across her pillow, she was like a little angel spreading her wings. I felt desperately sad but thankful at the same time. As it always did, Bernie's worsening situation had made me value my family.

The next day I called Linda. 'How's Bernie?' I asked.

'She's not good, Col,' Linda said. 'She had a coughing fit in the night and they've admitted her to Blackpool Vic. The doctors are giving her oxygen and morphine but they say they want to do more tests.'

The next day or two passed in a blur. I seemed to be constantly on the phone to Blackpool – and Bernie's condition was worsening by the hour. At five past three on the Tuesday afternoon I was sitting in the car outside Ciara's school, waiting to pick her up and drive her home, when Linda called again.

'I'm so sorry, Col, but you need to come now. Bernie's dying,' she said.

At that moment, the car door opened and Ciara was standing there. I must have looked as if I'd seen a ghost. All I could think of was that I had to get to Blackpool, and fast.

'Mum? Are you OK? What's happened?' Ciara was asking me.

'It's Auntie Bernie, love. She's not well at all,' I told her, trying not to show panic in my voice. 'Hop in quickly. I need to get home.'

I can't remember driving back but somehow I followed our familiar route through the twisting country lanes and screeched to a halt outside the house. I ran inside, threw a toothbrush into a bag and headed out to the car again.

Suddenly Ciara was crying. 'I want to come, Mum,' she said. 'If Auntie Bernie is so ill I want to come with you.'

I didn't have the strength to argue. Besides, she was probably right. If Bernie was about to die Ciara had a right to say her goodbyes, too. I nodded and, still wearing her school uniform, she jumped into the passenger seat of the car. We headed for Blackpool.

By the time I reached Blackpool Victoria Hospital, a breast-care nurse had already taken Steve to one side and gently told him that they were at an 'end of life' situation. Linda met Ciara and me in the waiting room for families and put her arms around me.

'They've given her two weeks,' she said quietly.

I couldn't believe what I was hearing. And suddenly I felt very angry. 'Hold on, she's gone from not curable but treatable to having a meal out on Saturday to being given two weeks to live? What the hell is going on?' I shouted.

Linda told me that the doctors believed Bernie's lungs were closing down. They wanted to move her to Trinity Hospice, where she would be more comfortable, for what little time she had left. Poor Steve and Bernie had been forced to break the news to their daughter, Erin. My heart ached for them.

Once Linda had taken Erin back to her house, Bernie insisted on starting to make plans for her funeral. She wanted to be buried in Blackpool with our parents and Kate, her stillborn daughter. Feisty Bernie even found the strength to look for poems she wanted read on the day. Poor Steve. I think he found that extremely difficult.

I phoned Ray back in Wilmslow. 'I'm not coming home,' I told him. 'If she's only got two weeks, that's how long I'm staying.'

'God, Col, I can't believe it,' he said. 'I'm coming over. I'll pick up Ciara and see Bernie at the same time.' He didn't voice it, but I knew Ray needed to say his own goodbyes.

The next day Bernie was moved to Trinity Hospice. It's a place you pray you never see the inside of but, it has to be said, it has a wonderful atmosphere and the staff are amazing. Bernie was given a beautiful room vast enough to fit in the army of family and friends who flocked from all over the country to see her. The lovely nurses didn't seem to mind who was there or for how long. They brought us cups of tea and let us stay overnight whenever we wanted. At times there must have been about forty people in that room, all there for one reason. Because they loved Bernie. I know that touched her.

Most of the family still live in Blackpool and they all gathered around. Of course, that meant Anne and Denise, too. I hadn't seen either of them for ages so it could have been awkward, but it never entered my head to say a cross word. We were all there for Bernie. We were brothers and sisters and they had as much right as I did to show her how much they loved her.

Those days in the hospice were surreal. Bernie was able to sit up and talk and her voice had gone up ten octaves. She was trying so hard to be normal but she just didn't sound like herself. I remember sitting, surrounded by my family and Bernie's friends, thinking how surreal it was. We were all together, trying to have a nice time but in two weeks I knew she would be dead.

We were sitting alone one night. 'Are you scared of dying?' I asked her. It had been preying on my mind and I was desperate to know her answer.

'Do you know? I'm not. I'm fucking angry, but I'm not scared,' she whispered. Christ, I would have been. I'd have wanted to be dosed up with morphine so I didn't know a thing about it.

'When I go, you'll cry,' she said. 'But after that I want you to get over it and get on with your life.' That was the first time I had to leave the room. I walked out and one of the nurses wrapped her arms around me. I sobbed and sobbed and sobbed. I was so moved by Bernie's matter-of-factness, her ability to just get on with it. I never once saw her cry. I know she did because I've since read her book – and it upset me more than I can say to know she wept privately – but she was always strong for us.

A few days later I was having a cup of tea in the waiting area when I heard Steve pick up a call from Bernie's breast-care nurse at the Royal Surrey, the hospital near their home that was providing her main treatment. I could hear him saying, 'You what?' He was obviously extremely agitated and he walked off into Reception where his signal was better. The next thing he rushed back into the room. 'They've got it wrong!' he shouted at anyone and everyone who could hear him. 'She hasn't only got two weeks! It's treatable!' Honestly, it was so dramatic it was like a scene out of a soap opera. In fact, you'd have thought it far-fetched if you'd watched it on *EastEnders*.

It turned out that Bernie had something called lymphangitis, which is an inflammation of the lymph vessels. It's caused by the cancer spreading and makes it difficult to breathe. No wonder she had been so ill. Lymphangitis was still very bad news but it was treatable with steroids. It seemed the hospital in Blackpool had assumed Bernie's deterioration was down to the progression of the cancer. Had she been admitted to a hospital that was more familiar with her condition, her doctors would have known to look for something else.

Once the hospice started giving her the right drugs, Bernie's condition improved rapidly. It felt as if she'd been given a reprieve and we were ecstatic. But while we didn't want to dampen Steve's enthusiasm, his expectations needed to be managed. He was saying things like, 'We could all still be here in ten years' time,' and we knew, sadly, that that was unlikely.

In Blackpool, Bernie was surrounded by a tight knot of family and friends, a support network that would be there for her and for Steve and Erin. It seemed sensible to us that she should stay at the hospice while she was having her treatment. But Bernie was having none of it. She yearned to go home: she wanted her own bed and she was worried about Erin missing so much time at school.

There were a few squabbles – as there often are with so many Nolans wanting their say. We felt Bernie and Steve would be isolated so far from the rest of the family and we wanted to be close to them. But Steve was adamant. 'You know what Bernie's like,' he said. 'She's such a fighter and she won't give up easily – she's going to be with us for a long time yet.' They were both determined, if the doctors would agree, to get back home to Weybridge.

So far, through the entire process of Bernie's breast cancer, from her initial diagnosis to her recovery, her setback and her brush with death, I'd been constantly overwhelmed by how kind people could be. Strangers would approach and ask how she was doing, ask me to pass on their good wishes and tell me they were praying for her. It really restored your faith in human nature. But now we were to be overwhelmed by a reaction of a very different sort.

Steve arranged for a friend to call into the house in Weybridge to make sure it was ready for Bernie's return. She would need a handrail in the bathroom and a lift for the stairs. When the friend let himself into the house he was appalled to find that burglars had ransacked it. While Bernie had been fighting for her life in Blackpool, the bastards had broken in and helped themselves to the keys to her beloved Saab convertible and the TV. They'd also been through each room, searching for valuables and leaving the place in a right mess.

We were utterly disgusted. Bernie's little family were already on their knees – it was the last thing they needed or deserved. I was due to visit Bernie that day at the hospice and I couldn't hide how furious I was. 'I can't believe anyone would do that, Bernie,' I said.

Amazingly, she wasn't that bothered. 'It's only stuff,' she said. I suppose, when your life hangs in the balance, everything else finds its own perspective. At that point, though, she didn't know what else had gone – there was worse to come.

Steve arranged for the house to be cleaned up before Bernie could see it. They travelled home together in an ambulance, not knowing what to expect. When Steve finally took stock of the damage he realized the thieves had smashed the lock on a little memory box in the front room in which they'd kept mementoes of their stillborn daughter, Kate. In their search for valuables, the burglars had emptied it out on to the floor, scattering photographs and the tiny bracelet Kate had worn in hospital. They'd also taken an engraved watch Bernie had given to Steve on their wedding day. He never got it back, although Bernie would later spend weeks scouring the internet to find an exact replica. She had it engraved with the words *Together until the end* and gave it to him on what was to prove their final wedding anniversary together.

Bernie was able to move on and concentrate on spending time with Steve and Erin, but the rest of the family found it more difficult to forget – and there was no way on God's earth that we would forgive. I still think the burglars must have been people who knew the family. They knew they were away and would not be back to disturb them. Even if they'd merely read it in the newspapers, it's still a miserable thing to do.

That sort of behaviour makes me sick. I hate the type of evil scumbag who is too lazy to earn their own money so they nick other people's stuff instead. There aren't many times when I despair of the human race but this was one of them. There are some toerags in this world.

With Bernie back home, we all tried to get on with our lives as best we could. She had good days and bad. I'd text her and wouldn't get a response and for a few days I'd be racked with worry. Then she'd text me asking if I could get a deal at a hotel in Blackpool for August! *Play the cancer card and they might give us a suite*, she'd joke.

*Bernie, you're not still playing that old card, are you? You're a disgrace!* I'd text back. I had to admire her chutzpah. Only Bernie could be so unwell and still be doggedly planning her summer holidays.

It was around this time that she decided she wanted to write her book. *Now and Forever* was to be her legacy to Erin and a love letter to Steve. She hated the thought that she would be known for ever as Cancer Girl. 'I'm a wife, mother, daughter, singer, actress, sister, friend and auntie,' she'd say. 'Those are the roles I want to define me.'

By May the book was written but Bernie was too ill to promote it. The task fell to me and my sisters: we had to get out there and do it for her. I was invited on to *This Morning* to talk about Bernie's story and it almost killed me to sit there on the sofa and tell Holly and Phillip how ill she was. As I sat in the makeup room I thought about all the happier times I had spent on the show. I don't want to be here promoting Bernie's last work, I thought. But she didn't have a voice, so I had to.

'Bernie's been amazing and so strong for all of us,' I told Holly and Phillip. 'She's written this book right up to the point where she couldn't any more, then Steve took over.'

I also explained to them that Bernie had been worried about letting down the other women in her situation. 'She feels that she's been telling them to be strong and not give up the fight – a fight that she may now lose. She doesn't want them to think that because her cancer has come back it's going to happen to them too,' I said. 'Bernie doesn't want them to give up.'

Again I had an overwhelming response. Bernie's illness really seemed to touch a lot of people. Old fans, new ones, people who hadn't ever followed the Nolans but found Bernie's story so very sad. I was inundated with lovely, lovely letters and emails. And when *Now and Forever* was published, it was a number-one bestseller.

At the end of May, Linda called. She'd gone to see Bernie and was shocked by what she'd found. The steroids were having an awful effect on her – her stomach was bloated and her face looked like she had cotton wool in her cheeks. 'I don't want to put pressure on anyone but I think she's deteriorating massively. It's time to get down there,' she said.

I knew that Ciara would want to see her auntie Bernie so the two of us headed to Surrey. 'Have you thought about what Auntie Bernie will look like?' I asked. Ciara had never seen anyone so ill before and I was worried about what we'd find. If things had deteriorated I wanted to protect her from the shock. But when we arrived, Bernie wasn't that bad. She was on oxygen and needed a wheelchair to get around, which was sad to see, but it was a relief not to find an altogether more distressing scene.

'It's so good to see you, Ciara!' Bernie said. 'Erin's been looking forward to it. She's in her bedroom playing on her Xbox. Go and find her.'

Ciara skipped off and, as I bent down to give her a hug, I could see the same old Bernie sparkle in her eyes. 'I'm fine, I'm fine,' she whispered, waving away my concern.

It was so lovely having a girly weekend together. Bernie and Erin. Me and Ciara. We ordered a takeaway, changed into our pyjamas and squashed together on the sofa to watch movies. 'Could you not get any closer, Ciara?' Bernie laughed, as her niece all but sat on her knee. I could tell Ciara wanted her fill of Bernie while she could. I'm so glad we had that time. It was good to see her.

As the summer continued it became clear to all of us that Bernie's fight couldn't last much longer. Linda and my brothers Brian and Tommy had planned to spend the weekend of 29 June with her. They said it was a great few days, with Steve surprising Bernie by secretly inviting the cast of *Chicago* to sing for her. They'd danced into the house singing 'Give Them The Old Razzle Dazzle'. She'd loved it. It was, however, to be her final party. On Monday, 1 July, Linda called and told me that Bernie probably had just days left. This time I didn't want to take Ciara with me. She'd said her goodbyes and spent her last visit with Auntie Bernie on the sofa. At twelve, she didn't need to see her die. Plus, she was due to go away on a school trip that day – it was kinder to put her on the coach and let her go off without a care.

Meanwhile the entire Nolan clan was mobilizing. The girls, my brothers, my nieces and nephews were all making their way down south. I met my niece, Tommy's daughter Laura, at Manchester Piccadilly so that I could travel with her on the train. After so many false alarms, it still felt unlikely that this would be the real thing. Knowing Bernie, I thought, we'll get there and she'll be sitting in the living room watching the football.

I gave Laura a hug and we climbed aboard. Linda kept texting me, asking where we were. I could tell by the panic in her messages that things were bad and

I hated the thought of Bernie dying before I could see her. When Linda texted me for about the twentieth time to tell us to hurry up, I thought I would explode.

*I'm only a passenger on this train. I'm not driving the bloody thing!* I told her.

When Laura and I reached Bernie's, Steve met us at the door and told us that she'd been sedated and was asleep upstairs. The night before they'd all been playing charades until one in the morning, and Steve had been fussing over her, asking Bernie if she wanted him to take her turn for her. Typical Bernie, she'd shouted at him, 'I've got fucking cancer, I'm not paralysed!' Then he'd stuck out his tongue behind her back and she was shouting, 'I can see you, you know!' They'd gone to bed but at six Bernie had woken up and started screaming. For three hours she'd screamed the house down. Linda said she and my brothers were standing in the kitchen with their hands over their ears, trying to block out Bernie's pain. In the end the nurse had dosed her up on morphine and now she was sleeping peacefully in her room.

'Go up and see her if you want to,' said Steve. I took off my coat and put it on top of the pile already lying on the sofa. So many people wanted to be there, it seemed. As I climbed the stairs and made my way to Bernie's bedroom I was anxious about how I'd find her. Linda's words about her screaming in the night had made my blood run cold. I tapped on the door gently and walked in. I needn't have worried. Bernie was sound asleep. She looked peaceful, not a sign of pain on her face. But she also looked tiny in her bed. As though part of her had already left us.

I sat down in the chair next to her bed, held her hand and stroked her hair. 'Hi, Bernie, it's Coleen,' I whispered. I didn't want to wake her but I wanted her to know I was there. 'Thought I'd better come and see what trouble you're causing now.' I half expected her to open her eyes and say, 'What are you doing here? I'm fine!' But, of course, she didn't. It seemed we'd probably had the last of our false alarms, but I desperately hoped we hadn't.

I went downstairs and saw there were around sixteen of us in the house. Over the next few hours we slept in shifts and made huge rounds of tea and toast to keep everyone going. Upstairs we sang to Bernie and talked for hours around the clock. I hoped she could hear us, chatting happily, all the feuds and petty arguments forgotten. Nothing mattered now except our beautiful sister.

There was a large television in Bernie's bedroom and we switched it on to break the terrible hush. I remember it was the time of the men's tennis quarter finals at Wimbledon and Andy Murray was playing Fernando Verdasco. Bernie had always loved sport and I kept telling her the score. When Murray won after five sets we were dancing around the room. If Bernie had woken up and joined us I wouldn't have been that shocked. It seems bizarre now.

*

On Thursday, 4 July, I was in the kitchen putting the kettle on for yet another pot of tea when Linda shouted for me to come upstairs. I ran up and found everybody looking really grave. Bernie's breathing had changed and we knew we were close to the end.

That final scene will stay with me for the rest of my life. Steve and Erin lay either side of Bernie on the bed and the rest of us girls got on to the bed too and lay where we could, holding on to her. I could hear Bernie breathing. Steve and Erin were talking to her, saying how much they loved her, and the rest of us were stroking her legs and arms. None of us was crying at that stage, not wanting to fill those last precious moments with tears.

Then Bernie's breathing changed again and she gave three little gasps . . . and was gone. Briefly, there was a wailing wall of hysteria. We all wanted to comfort Erin, but the crying that we'd so far managed to hold back could be stifled no longer. We wept in each other's arms, howling like injured animals. After a few moments it was as if the storm had passed and we were calm.

In its way it was a beautiful death. It sounds crazy but Bernie would have loved it. She was surrounded by the most important people in her life, wrapped up in love and sent on her way. Afterwards we played her album and sat with her, listening to the music. It was just so lovely, it couldn't have been any better.

People behave very differently in grief. My own reaction was to sit quietly with a cup of tea, but Steve was almost manic. He raced around the house putting on Bernie's CDs and having her voice blaring out in every room. He was inconsolable.

We let the immediate family and friends know, and we warned Neil, but we decided we would keep the news private initially, while we tried to start to come to terms with it in our own time. But, unfortunately, within thirty minutes the press frenzy had begun. The actress Lisa Riley had put out a message of condolence on Twitter. *RIP Bernie! We had such a laugh when we worked together! The angels are waiting for you, as is my mum with a large glass! Always in our hearts. Xxxx* This tweet started a chain reaction of phone calls from around the world, people wanting quotes and to find out the facts surrounding Bernie's death. I'm sure Lisa did it unwittingly but it opened the floodgates and meant the world's press suddenly knew that Bernie had gone. It also meant that Neil had to call Linda and me to warn us that the news had leaked out. He then had no choice but to disturb Bernie's husband, Steve, moments after her death to warn him. It was devastating and I'm sure Lisa would be appalled to realize the impact one tweet had. She lost her mother to cancer a few years ago and is a truly lovely girl.

People who had admired Bernie started to use Twitter to share their grief. *Just heard the very sad news that gorgeous, courageous and inspirational Bernie Nolan has died. Big love to all the family x,* said Phillip Schofield. *Bernie Nolan was a very special woman. Brave, funny and hugely talented. She will be sorely missed. Thoughts with her family and friends,* said Lorraine Kelly. Jennifer Ellison, whom Bernie had worked with on *Brookside,* tweeted, *So sad to hear Bernie Nolan has passed away! Such an amazing lady, had the honour of working with her twice will cherish the memories x.* My old pal Sherrie Hewson wrote, *RIP the wonderfully talented Bernie Nolan, a beautiful person that lit up this sometimes dark world of ours! Sing forever Bernie! X.* I especially liked the tweet from actor Joe McGann, who had starred with Bernie in *Calendar Girls.* He said, *RIP Bernie Nolan – Fabulous voice, funny, generous pocket-amazon I was lucky to have known.* Love just poured on to the site.

Then the phone was ringing off its hook. Reporters wanting to know if it was true, wanting to ask how we felt and if we wanted to give a quote for the newspapers. We felt as if we were under siege.

I called Ray to tell him what had happened so he didn't hear it first on the TV. Of course, he was heartbroken and felt helpless because he wasn't able to comfort me. That was when I heard about the press release that Neil had had to put together quickly. Ray read it to me: 'Bernie passed away peacefully this morning with all of her family around her. The entire family are devastated to have lost beloved Bernie. A wonderful wife, adoring mother and loving sister, she is irreplaceable. They kindly ask people to respect their privacy at this difficult time.'

I don't think any of us expected Bernie's death to attract such a massive amount of press interest. Every TV channel, every paper, every magazine and radio bulletin seemed to lead with the news. Some of the family resented the intrusion but I didn't, and I know Bernie wouldn't have minded. She lived her whole life in the public eye and you can't do that and then complain when the public is interested in you. I know how it works and, although it was overwhelming, every single piece that went out was just beautiful.

The next morning the tributes poured in. Jesus, it was comforting. I was only sorry that she couldn't feel the rush of affection. I don't think she ever grasped how popular she was and how much she was loved by her fans and the people in the business she'd worked with.

Suddenly I was desperate to get back to my own family. I knew Shane Junior was at home with Ray and I needed to be with them. The journey gave me some peace and time to think and I felt very calm. I urged the car to get me home as fast as possible. I was still calm as I put my key in the door and hauled my bag into the hall. Then I walked into my kitchen, put my arms around Shane and absolutely broke my heart again.

'I'm so sorry, Mum,' he soothed. I let myself stay in the arms of my boy and cried for what seemed a very long time.

For the next few days the most trivial things set me off. Just washing the dishes or making a cup of tea felt wrong because they were things that Bernie was never going to do again. I'd sit down to watch telly only to find I couldn't concentrate on the programme. Who cares? I'd think. Nothing matters because Bernie has died. I'd be having my evening meal with Shane and Ray, lift the fork to my mouth and break down again. Nothing seemed right.

Ciara was still away on her school trip and I was terrified she'd hear the news of Bernie's death before I could tell her myself. We phoned the school secretary and she got in touch with the teachers at their hotel to warn them. They were brilliant. They explained that where they were in Wales there was no mobile phone signal and that the news had not reached Ciara. On the coach home they collected all the kids' phones and wouldn't give them back until they arrived.

'Let's not tell her immediately,' I said to Ray. 'She'll be so excited about her trip, I can't bear to burst her bubble.'

Ciara was happy to see us and we whisked her straight off to McDonald's for a burger. For the next two hours she didn't stop chattering about the holiday. Then, out of the blue, she just said, 'How's Auntie Bernie?'

'Auntie Bernie died a couple of days ago, darling,' I told her gently.

She walked over to me and gave me a hug. 'I'm so happy we went to see her while she was still OK,' she said. 'I'd like to remember her like that.' She handled it brilliantly and I was very proud of her. I know how much she loved her auntie Bernie.

When somebody you love dies you're bound to be left with a lot of questions. They say that anger is one of the five stages of grief, and I've definitely been through times when I've felt furious about Bernie's death. I only found out recently that when Bernie had her initial surgery the doctors kept her nipple and used it in the breast reconstruction that she was having there and then.

Over and over again I keep comparing Bernie's surgery against Linda's. When Linda was diagnosed she had a full mastectomy, followed by chemotherapy. Nothing was left. She had a flat chest with a neat four-inch scar. It was ages afterwards that she had a reconstruction. With Bernie, she was given chemo first and then the mastectomy followed. As we now know, while she was asleep on the operating table they tested her nipple, found it was clear of cancer and so saved it. But why was their treatment so different?

The fact that the cancer came back is also difficult to come to terms with. It seems so unfair that Bernie was pronounced cancer free, only for it to come back even more aggressively. It makes me very angry. Bernie was only fifty-two. The whole thing just seems so unfair.

Losing Bernie punched a big hole in the Nolan family. It felt like a huge chunk of it was missing. It does even now, months down the line. Every time there's a family get-together I'm reminded that she's gone. There was a birthday party for one of Anne's daughters recently and it felt so strange not to see Bernie, a glass of vodka in her hand, kicking off the singing. Linda felt it too, I know. She walked over to me as I was getting teary and put her arms around me.

'Come on, she wouldn't want this,' she said.

I didn't see Bernie that regularly but we'd text a lot and I carry on my days like she's still in Surrey. Something was troubling me the other day and I thought, I know, I'll ask Bernie. I was driving the car and I got to the traffic lights and suddenly remembered that I couldn't. I sat there, long after the lights had turned green, feeling the loss wash through me all over again.

When I really need her I watch our I'm In The Mood Again tour DVD. There's Bernie, belting out her songs, putting us all to shame with her amazing vocals. Linda, Maureen and I have our moments but Bernie was undoubtedly the star of the show. Her personality jumps out of the screen and is infectious. It's all I can do to stop myself dancing along with her. Thank God for that tour, is all I can say. There were so many times when it nearly didn't happen, but it did and it was magical for all of us. It was meant to be.

# Chapter Ten

The two weeks after Bernie's death were completely surreal. It was as if we were planning a wedding, not a funeral. There were cars to be booked and flowers to be organized. People kept calling the house and asking if it was a private ceremony and whether they could come and pay their respects.

Everywhere I went strangers would approach and tell me how they loved Bernie and how sorry they were to hear about her death. I was in Waitrose when a woman stopped me and said that she, too, had lost her sister to breast cancer and that she knew how I felt. There was a shared acknowledgement of grief, then she picked up her shopping basket and walked off down the tinned-veg aisle. I met a lot of very lovely people during that time.

'A GRIEVING COLEEN NOLAN RUNS ERRANDS AS SHE PREPARES TO LAY HER SISTER BERNIE TO REST,' screamed the *Daily Mail*, alongside several photographs of a woman in dark glasses walking like a zombie in a car park behind a shopping trolley. Bloody hell, what did they expect? My beautiful sister was dead but we still had to eat. I still had to get up every morning and take Ciara to school. I still had to feed my family and take the dogs out for a run.

When I look back on those pictures now I see a woman on autopilot, just trying to get through her day. To be honest, I don't even remember being in the supermarket, it's all a blank. Occasionally I'll get flashbacks to that period, but the scenes are like something off the television – I don't recognize the woman in them.

Scenes such as me standing in front of the washing machine, just staring out of the window with tears streaming down my face. 'Coleen?' Ray would say, to gently bring me back. 'You've been standing there for ages not doing anything. Do you want me to wash the pots?'

'No, it's fine. I'm fine,' I'd say. Each time I stand at the sink I relive that scene over and over again.

Another recurring flashback of Bernie is the one I have every time I go to text my brother, Brian. His name is just below Bernie's on my phone. I still have her number – why would I delete it? Just seeing her name on the screen makes me so sad that I can forget what I was doing and simply stand there, phone in hand.

What I do remember is feeling guilty for being out and about. Ray would offer to go for me but what else was I going to do? I couldn't just sit in the house and cry. Ray was unbelievable over those two weeks. When he needs to be, there's no one better for me than him. He took Ciara to school, he looked after the horses, nipped out for shopping – wherever I needed him to be, there he was. After our earlier difficulties it made me thank God that we had made it through. When somebody close to you dies it makes you realize that life's too short to worry about how many times you've been hugged that day. Although, to be fair to Ray, during that period he was giving out hugs to anybody who needed one.

There were days when I couldn't face getting out of bed and I was glad to let Ray take over. But in the end I had to haul myself from under the duvet and get dressed. I've seen too many people with depression – I know how it kicks in. I had to find that little part of me that said, Whether or not you want to, you're getting up and you have to get up now!

It made me think back to my mum and the rest of her generation. When I was growing up I'd see her upset and frustrated by my dad's behaviour but she never felt sorry for herself. She just got up and did what she had to do to take care of us eight kids. Since Linda lost her Brian she's suffered really badly with depression. She'll tell you herself that at one stage she even phoned the Samaritans for help. But my mum and Ray's mum, Irene, who were married for fifty years and then left totally alone, just got on with it. My mum was heartbroken but she got up and did the shopping. Ray's mum sometimes says, 'Oh, I miss my Sid every day,' but I've never seen her cry. She's never been on anti-depressants, she's never had counselling. There's something about that generation of women that makes them much tougher than we are.

Besides, in the back of my head I could hear my bossy sister screaming at me, 'Jesus, Col, just get a bloody move on!'

Bernie had wanted to be cremated at Carleton Crematorium in Blackpool, where our parents and her daughter Kate had been cremated. But the building was undergoing some renovations, which meant the funeral couldn't happen immediately. Those two weeks were so painful. I felt as if I was waiting and waiting for the worst day of my life. I was dreading it but at the same time wanting the day to arrive. Until a funeral takes place it's as if you can't grieve properly. Afterwards you can say, 'OK. Now life goes on,' but up to that point you haven't really said goodbye. Bernie was with us all, keeping us strong, reminding us to carry on, but still it was hard.

Thank God she'd arranged everything before she died. When the Nolans get together to plan an event there will be inevitable squabbles and fall-outs, but with Bernie's instructions ringing in our ears there was no chance of that. She'd told us who was sitting with whom in the funeral cars, what music was to be played and which readings would be used. She'd planned everything down to the smallest detail, but the one big decision still to be made was where to hold the service.

Bernie was adamant that she didn't want it held in a church and had left instructions to have the service at the crematorium. It soon became clear, though, that this wasn't going to be possible. The crematorium can hold about a hundred people, tops, and, by now, it was obvious there would be many more who wanted to pay their respects. We looked around for suitable venues but everywhere was either too small or too churchy.

One night, we were sitting round at Maureen's house when her husband Ritchie suddenly made the perfect suggestion: Blackpool's Grand Theatre! It seemed so fitting. It was the showbiz heart of the town we'd grown up in and it was a theatre we loved and had performed in so many times. I could almost see Bernie jumping up and down and shouting, 'Yes!'

'Oh, my God, that's so perfect, Ritchie,' said Linda. 'She would have loved that.'

Finally, the day arrived. Ciara had another school trip planned, this time to Paris, and, to be honest, it was a relief. I knew Bernie wouldn't have wanted her to miss her holiday and it meant I didn't have to worry about her on the day. It would just be me, Ray, the boys, friends and family – and the whole of Blackpool!

We drove from Wilmslow the night before and stayed with lots of other relatives and friends at the Carousel Hotel, which is close to the seafront on South Shore. That night was all about Bernie. We had a few drinks, told stories about her life and took some time to think about her.

'Do you remember when we went with them to Rome and Bernie was sozzled and sang the theme to *The Godfather* out of the window?' said my brother, Brian, to his wife, Annie.

'Oh, my God, yes. She belted it out so well that by the time she was finished there must have been two hundred people standing in the piazza listening to her!'

laughed Annie. 'I've still got that on film somewhere. She was amazing.'

We filled our glasses and toasted our golden girl. 'Let's have another round,' I heard myself say. I felt like I never wanted to go to bed because I dreaded what the following day would bring.

The next morning I woke early and could see already that we were going to get the most beautiful weather. The sun poured into the bedroom and outside there was barely a breath of cloud to break up the cornflower-blue sky. I was tempted to dive back under the duvet but, again, the autopilot kicked in. It had to: without it, I doubt I'd have been able to get up and dressed.

Everything seemed so strange. I was putting on my outfit, slipping my arms into a sparkly black jacket, when I thought, What am I doing? This can't be right. I did my hair, put on some makeup, looked at myself in the mirror and thought, Who cares what I look like? It really doesn't matter. But of course, it did. Bernie would want us to put on a show.

I stepped outside the hotel for a cigarette and there, all dressed from head to toe completely in black, were about a dozen family members. Suddenly I felt quite hysterical and burst out laughing. 'Do you reckon anyone driving by would guess what we're doing today?' I said. It's bizarre how moments of hilarity pop up like that to pierce the sombre mood. I suddenly realized that whenever there was a family gathering, it was usually Bernie who had organized it. For us all to be together without her felt odd.

The plan was for us to go to Brian's, where the cars would pick us up. We all trooped over there and knocked on the door. Brian answered, looking smart in his grey suit and white shirt. We had a hug and I could feel him trembling. Everyone seemed very nervous. I've been to lots of funerals – I've lost my mum and dad and other relatives – but this was different. My hands were shaking and I felt dizzy. From the look of everyone else, I wasn't alone.

Suddenly I heard someone say, 'The cars are here,' and that really was the very worst moment for me. There's something about seeing your loved one's coffin for the first time that is shocking and absolutely tears at your heart. We walked outside and there was the most beautiful shiny black vintage hearse. Behind its gleaming windows was Bernie's coffin, covered with deep red roses and snowy lilies. I could see other floral tributes, spelling out 'Auntie' and 'Sister'. Pride of place was a simple arrangement that simply said, 'Mum'. Poor Erin.

My encounter with the old fortune-teller on Venice Beach seemed like a million years ago but now, just over a year later, it came back to haunt me. She had warned that Ray would be hit hard by Bernie's death. 'Your husband is going to be amazing,' she said. 'He'll support you every step of the way but he'll fall apart when she dies.' And now here it came. When Ray set eyes on the car carrying Bernie he was the first to weep. After a few moments he wiped his eyes and was furious with himself for breaking down.

'I should be strong for you,' he said.

I gave him a hanky from my handbag and told him not to be so daft. 'She was important to you too, Ray. It's allowed,' I said.

Pretty soon after that it was my turn to fall apart. Alongside the cars, a police escort had pulled up outside the house. Two bikes and a police car were alongside the funeral cortège and that really got to me. It hinted that we were on very public show and that we'd be joined by crowds of onlookers. I hadn't expected that and it underlined the enormity of what we were doing there that day.

We climbed into the cars – following Bernie's instructions as to who sat where and with whom – and slowly followed the hearse on the journey to the Grand. Then we saw for the first time something that was to be repeated throughout the day. People, complete strangers, were lining the pavements, their hands across their chests, their heads bowed. We drove past some roadworks and the men took off their hard hats and bowed their heads. We went past shops and people came out and bowed their heads. The worst, the absolute worst for me, was when we went past a homeless man wearing an old beanie hat – he reached up, removed it and lowered his head. For some reason that touched me more than anything.

Then we turned the corner into the main shopping area and we were met by a wall of sound. There must have been thousands of people all respectfully applauding as the cars swept by. In our car Linda, Ray,

Jake, Shane and his girlfriend Emma went to pieces. I did, too. It was overwhelming. We'd never expected the funeral to prompt such a reaction from so many. But we should have. It was clear they had been touched by Bernie's story and they wanted to be part of the day. The showbiz star in her would have loved it.

It may have felt a little intrusive for some, but it wasn't for Bernie. It was fantastic for her. It was like a mini Diana funeral all over again. People were throwing flowers on to the hearse, clapping their hands and shouting out their feelings. I wanted her to see it. I felt like knocking on her coffin and shouting, 'See this? Do you see how much you're loved?'

By now we had reached the Grand, where the family had planned to meet in a little bar at the back of the theatre. Everybody else had to go through the main entrance – but they would only be allowed in if they knew a secret password.

This, too, had caused hilarity. Someone – possibly Brian or my other brother Tommy – had decided the password should be 'Bonzo'. It was our nickname for Bernie when we were younger and a name she used for her own Bonzo music publishing company. One of our friends, Mark, who I'm often winding up, phoned to ask for the password so that he could get into the theatre.

'It's Bonzo,' I told him.

'Fuck off. If you think I'm going up to a policeman at Bernie's funeral and saying, "Bonzo" you're crazy,' he said.

'I'm serious,' I said. 'That's the password.'

'Look, Coleen, it's just not funny this time. I've known Bernie for years and I've never heard anyone call her Bonzo.' By now he sounded quite distressed.

'Well, Mark, say what you want but you won't get in unless you use the password,' I said.

When he found out I was telling the truth he texted me back to say he was sorry.

I was standing with Ray at the tiny theatre bar when Anne walked in. She and I had spoken at Brian's house and shared a hug, but it had been years since she and Ray had been civil to one another. There was no avoiding it: she had to brush past him to get through and, suddenly, all the years of animosity and resentment were washed away.

'Hello, you,' he said, and hugged her.

She hugged him back and burst into tears. Before long all three of us were bawling and she walked away to see her daughters. I could hear her saying, 'Ray's just hugged me!' It was an emotional moment and he handled it brilliantly. He's not a bad lad.

By now the theatre seats had filled and it was time to go in. Bernie's coffin was to be carried by Shane Junior, Maureen's son Danny, my nephew Tommy Junior and my two brothers. Jake was asked if he wanted to carry it, too, but he couldn't face it. 'I'm sorry, Mum,' he said. 'I just couldn't.' I understood and was proud of him for being so honest.

But now Shane was about to go into the lobby to

have the coffin lowered on to his shoulders and he was absolutely terrified. I could see his hands trembling.

'Look, Shane, if you can't do this it's not a problem. There are pallbearers ready to step in if you feel wobbly,' I told him.

But he shook his head. Bernie was his godmother and they were very close. 'I've got to do it,' he said. I kissed his cheek. My little boy seemed more of a man than ever.

As we walked into the packed theatre to take our seats I could see so many familiar faces. Tommy Cannon and Bobby Ball were there, Roy Walker, Joe Longthorne, Roy 'Chubby' Brown and Ray Quinn. I could even see my ex-husband, Shane Richie, sitting with his mum in the stalls. Shane had been a part of our family, he was Bernie's brother-in-law and, as dad to my boys, I was glad to have him there.

I spotted my sister Denise sitting at the front next to Anne. We hadn't spoken at Brian's house and now she was weeping quietly, her hands held to her face. I walked to where she sat, put my arms around her and we hugged. It seemed the natural thing to do. Ray and I sat down a few seats away from her, Linda between us, and the music began.

The enormous stage was set very simply. A huge screen hung on the backdrop while a single spotlight shone down on a beautiful display of lilies and the empty trestle on which the coffin would be placed. Slowly, the boys carried Bernie in and placed her down.

A fabulous picture of her filled the screen. She was centre stage one last time.

My brother Brian welcomed the guests. 'Today is obviously a tragic day and very sad,' he said. 'But this is also a celebration of a life beautifully lived. Bernie was an incredible person. We will cry obviously, but please understand it is OK to smile and laugh today, because that is what she would have wanted.'

Next up was Maureen, who somehow managed to read aloud a letter that Bernie had written for the service. My heart raced as I watched her take her place. I was full of admiration – there was no way I could have done that.

'"Hello, everybody, and thank you for coming,"' said Maureen, reading out our sister's words. '"Don't be crying too much for me. Obviously I'd like a bit. I think I'm worth a little crying, but not too much.

'"No one has had a better life than me really, fifty years of singing some of the best ever shows, including *Chicago*, *Blood Brothers*, *The Sound of Music*, *My Fair Lady* and *City of Angels*. What an amazing time I have had.

'"By the age of nineteen I had been all over the world, sung with Stevie Wonder, toured with Frank Sinatra . . . Do not mourn my passing, CELEBRATE my wonderful life.

'"I have the most wonderful family who have supported me always, giving me great advice and constant love. As for my husband and daughter – how did I get so lucky?

'"Steve has been my constant rock, misunderstood

terribly at times, but if only you all knew what he has done for me and how he has set up Erin's life so she won't ever have to worry again, how he has cared for me and basically given up so much for me.

'"Every seventeenth of October I want you to have a party, or at least a good old drink, for my birthday. Make it vodka."'

The letter was typical Bernie. People were crying and laughing all at the same time. The screen flashed with a slideshow of pictures: Bernie singing, Bernie giggling, Bernie with her beloved Steve and Erin, her 'two heroes', as she described them in the order of service that we were all clutching.

Then, showing she'd inherited every ounce of her mother's spirit and bravery, Erin stepped up. She read 'Do Not Stand at My Grave and Weep' by Mary Elizabeth Frye. I was so proud of her.

> Do not stand at my grave and weep,
> I am not there; I do not sleep.
> I am a thousand winds that blow,
> I am the diamond glints on snow,
> I am the sunlight on ripened grain,
> I am the gentle autumn rain.
> When you awaken in the morning's hush
> I am the swift uplifting rush
> Of quiet birds in circled flight.
> I am the soft stars that shine at night.
> Do not stand at my grave and cry,
> I am not there; I did not die.

How does a fourteen-year-old kid do that? Incredible. She put her auntie to shame. I was too chicken to do a reading. I knew I wouldn't manage it. But when it was Linda's turn to say her piece, she grabbed my hand and pulled me up with her. 'Just come and stand by me,' she whispered. I'm glad I did because when she lost it and started drying up I was able to gently urge her on.

'I want to tell you what an amazing sister Bernie was,' she said . . . and then went quiet.

'Just breathe,' I whispered.

She took a deep breath and went on: 'I miss her laugh, her smile, her words of encouragement. I miss her compassion and her never-ending lust for life. There will never, ever be another like her. Today we, her brothers and sisters, are broken. We miss you, Bernie.'

She then read from a poem called 'She Is Gone' by David Harkins, which ended with the words:

> You can cry and close your mind, be empty and
> turn your back
> Or you can do what she would want: smile, open
> your eyes, love and go on.

I held Linda's hand as we left the stage, glad to have taken some part in the proceedings.

The final part of the service was a video of Bernie at one of her concerts, singing Whitney Houston's 'Run To You'. It's a beautiful song and Bernie's version was just brilliant. It was great to hear her gorgeous, strong voice belting out one last time. When she was finished, the crowd at the concert went wild and she took a bow, looked out at us from beyond the screen and said simply, 'Goodnight and thank you.' It was fabulously done.

Until that moment I'd held it together, mainly by digging my fingernails into the fleshy bits of my hands. But seeing Bernie, going out exactly as she would have wanted and saying her goodbyes, was too much to bear. I remember thinking, I'm going to die here. I'm going to cry and cry and not be able to stop and in the end they'll have to carry me out. I had to have a word with myself.

I was leaning on Ray. He had his arm around me and was holding on tightly as I wept. It felt as if the stress and the grief that I'd been carrying ever since I knew Bernie's illness was going to take her from us was pouring out of me. I clung to Ray and, although he was supporting me, I could feel he was doing exactly the same. He stroked my head and let me cry until there was a break in the tears. Then, when it was time to leave the theatre, he helped me to my feet, taking my weight as I somehow walked up the aisle and out into the sunshine.

The streets were still full of people. There seemed to be even more than there had been on our journey to the theatre. The service had been relayed by public broadcast system to the waiting crowds and, as we climbed into the cars and headed to the crematorium, they applauded. Then they started cheering. On street after street they lined the pavements, throwing flowers and clapping their hands. It was extraordinary. Then we turned down Corporation Street and, as we drove past a bar called Scruffy Murphy's, we could hear Bernie singing 'I'm In The Mood For Dancing'. The landlord had directed speakers out of the windows and was playing it, full blast, on a loop. I held Ray's hand tightly and, as Bernie's voice filled the car, we smiled at one another.

After the crowds and razzmatazz of the public service, Carleton Crematorium felt very calm and peaceful. Only family and close friends had been invited to this part of the funeral and about a hundred of us sent Bernie on her way. Bernie's husband, Steve, was so heartbroken. It was terrible to see his pain. He stood up and fished in his pocket for the piece of paper on which he'd written his final love letter to his darling wife.

'Bernie radiated love, life and happiness,' he read out. 'She showed me what true love was and it was beautiful. Every day was an adventure and I just held on to her coat tails, and loved every second of it.

'I can't imagine life without her, and I still can't believe she's gone.' His voice, strong yet breaking, filled the crematorium. 'I know I was the luckiest man in the world to have loved and been loved by her. She gave us our beautiful daughter, who has been my strength through all of these dark days.

'She lit up every room she ever walked into, and she

lit up my life for ever. I'll love you for eternity, Bernie, my beautiful girl.'

I hoped she was watching her daughter and husband that day. Their words were full of love and grief but also happiness and gratitude for the time they'd had with her. She would have been very proud.

At one point I looked at Linda and I could see that she was losing control, just as I had done in the theatre. Seeing her so distressed kind of snapped me out of my misery and I rushed over to hold her up. It's funny how often that happens. It takes seeing someone else in a bad way to make you be strong.

I held Linda's arm as we slowly shuffled towards the front of the crematorium to file past the coffin one last time. Everybody touched the casket and whispered their goodbye. I leaned down, kissed the lid of the coffin and said, 'I love you, Bernie.' And that was that.

Steve had found a beautiful piece of music called 'My Wild Irish Rose', which seemed fitting because that's what she was. As we were leaving the crematorium and the music played out behind us, we were met by an amazing sight. Steve and Erin had planned to release some doves from a basket and one of the birds was refusing to come out. 'That's Bernie,' I said. 'She's not going anywhere until she's had a party!'

The lady who hired out the doves – usually for weddings – had declined any payment. 'I don't want any money,' she'd said. 'If you'd like it, I'll do it.' In fact she wasn't alone. The people who had supplied the video screens and the speakers did it for nothing, too. Most of them had worked with Bernie at one time or another and wanted to do their bit to help. It sounds cheesy, but when something awful happens it so often restores your faith in human nature. Everyone was just great.

And so, as Bernie had wanted, there followed the biggest of parties, this time at the Grand Hotel, where she'd married her Steve. It was a beautiful evening, though tinged massively with sadness. But by now we were all cried out and it was time to remember what she stood for. We had a band, people sang, we danced and raised a glass to our sister. From several huge screens her picture beamed out at us and every few minutes I'd remember why we were there. It was the celebration of her life she had asked for.

Back in February, when she was in the hospice and we thought we were going to lose her, she'd told me she wasn't frightened of dying. What really made her angry was that she was going to miss the party of her life. And on that night in Blackpool, as we finally finished partying at five in the morning, I felt the tears well up as I wished upon wish that it was a party we hadn't had to have.

# Chapter Eleven

The loss of Bernie was painful for all of us. But what was odd was the physical effect her death had on me.

During those final dark days I'd begun to notice a terrible itch on my hands. It was as if I'd plunged them into that itching powder us kids used to get from the joke shop in Blackpool. Whatever lotions I slathered on them, I couldn't make them feel any better. It was driving me mad.

'My hands are red raw with all this itching and scratching,' I told Ray one day, when I couldn't stand it any longer. 'I think I must be allergic to something.'

'Perhaps it's something down at the stables,' he said. 'You've always got your hands stuck in something revolting while you're mucking out the horses,' he joked. But I couldn't understand why it had so suddenly affected me. Then, a few days later when Ciara and I were at our local GP's surgery, the mystery was solved.

We'd gone because of some little health niggle she had, and while we were talking to the doctor, Ciara decided to take matters into her own hands. By now the itching had turned into hard, flaky skin and the ring finger on my right hand was in a terrible scabby mess.

'Show her your finger, Mum,' she said suddenly. I rolled my eyes, laughed and obediently held out my hand for inspection.

To my surprise, the doctor took it quite seriously. 'That's really nasty,' she said. 'It looks to me like eczema that's become infected. Do you usually suffer from it?' I told her I'd never had eczema in my life and that was when she hit the nail on the head. 'Have you been under any stress lately?' she asked.

I took a deep breath. 'My sister died two weeks ago,' I said quietly.

'That'll be it, then,' she said. Great, I thought. On top of everything else I've got scabby, infected eczema fingers.

Since then it's flared up regularly. On holiday in September it got into my eyes and I woke up looking like something out of a horror film. Whenever I'm stressed I know I'm going to get another attack. And so it proved during the next few months, which turned out to be very stressful indeed.

After Bernie died I received thousands and thousands of messages. It was overwhelming. No one else in the family is on Twitter – Steve especially loathes it – so I felt I had to share with them the great outpouring of grief and love that Bernie's death had prompted.

'You won't believe the things people are saying on Twitter,' I'd tell Steve. 'Bernie's story seems to have touched so many of them. I've had such gorgeous messages.' Sometimes I'd copy them and send them by email. They were a comfort to me and, I hoped, they would be to Steve and Erin, too.

But for the ninety-eight per cent of genuine and lovely folk you get on Twitter, there are the two per cent who are absolute morons. A couple of weeks after Bernie died – around the same time my eczema flared up – I had the following message: *Now that your sister's popped her clogs, hopefully you'll get cancer too and then you'll lose weight, you fat bitch.*

Usually, when I get the occasional rude tweet, I just block the sender and forget it. But this was different. Because they had mentioned Bernie I wanted to find whoever had sent it and kill them. Suddenly Twitter, the place where I'd gone for support and love, turned out to be a hostile and threatening environment.

I showed Ray. 'Can you believe people can be so revolting?' I said. It was probably the wrong thing to do because he hates all that stuff. It's beyond him why I bother with it.

'Close the bloody thing down, Col,' he said. 'The last thing you need at the moment is messages from arseholes like that.'

But the good point about Twitter is that sometimes you don't have to worry about responding – others do it for you. I have about 127,000 followers, the majority of whom are fiercely loyal and supportive. The moment they see an abusive post they leap on the sender like protective parents. Suddenly the moron who'd posted the tweet about Bernie was being bombarded with hundreds of irate messages. By the time they'd finished lashing out, I almost felt sorry for him. Almost. He must have been thinking, Jeez, leave me alone. I wish I'd never started this now. It was reassuring to know that there are genuine people out there who have your back.

One afternoon in August, I was in the house watching TV with Ciara and Ray. It had been a beautiful day; Ciara and I had been riding Paddy and Orla together, and it felt good to snuggle up with her on the sofa. Just then my phone pinged to show I had a Twitter message.

'COLEEN FENSOME,' it read, in large capital letters. Already my hackles were up – it was very unusual for anyone on Twitter to use my married name. It went on: 'A BOMB HAS BEEN PLACED OUTSIDE UR HOME AND IT WILL GO OFF @22.47 HRS ON A TIMER AND TRIGGER.' Oh, my God. I read it again. My hands shaking, I threw the phone on to the floor and instinctively pulled Ciara towards me. What should I do? It was obviously some nutter's idea of a joke, but targeting my home and family was certainly not funny.

'Stay here, Ciara,' I said. 'I just want to check something.' Quickly, I ran to the door and stepped outside on to the drive. I did a sweep of the garden and the area around the house. Nothing. I opened the gates and searched along the perimeter wall. Again, nothing.

I told Ray. 'For fuck's sake, Coleen,' he said. 'Block whoever sent it and don't look at the site again. Do you want to call the police?'

By now I'd calmed down quite a bit and I didn't want to give the moron the satisfaction of making the news. 'No, it's fine,' I said. 'I don't want to make a big thing of it. That's exactly what he wants.'

'OK, well, I'll check the locks and you try to relax,' instructed Ray. 'And don't look at that bloody site!'

That night Ciara slept with me in my bed. I hadn't told her about the message but I think she could tell that something had spooked me. We cuddled together, my arms wrapped tightly and protectively around her. As she slept I watched the red glowing numbers of my digital alarm clock. 22:45 . . . 22:46 . . . 22:47 . . . 22:48 . . . I hadn't realized how tense my body was until the clock clicked past 22:47. Only then did I feel my jaw and neck muscles begin to soften, my teeth unclench and my shoulders relax. At last I drifted off and the next thing I knew it was morning.

A day or so later I had the shock of my life when I read in the newspapers that two of the boys from Blue – Antony Costa and Duncan James – had gone to the police over a Twitter troll who had sent both of them bomb threats. But the chilling part was that the troll had mentioned a time when the bomb was set to go off – 22:47. It wasn't the same name on the account but it couldn't just be a coincidence, could it? I called my good friend Antony.

'What do you reckon? Do you think he's seen us tweeting one another and made a connection?' I asked him.

Antony wasn't sure, but he was very angry about it

because the message had mentioned his sister and mum. 'It's when they threaten your family that it really gets to you, isn't it?' he said. He was right. But I hoped that now, with the police involved, it would be the end of it.

The following day I was out shopping in Wilmslow. Ciara was at her friend's house and Ray was at home. I pulled into the car park in the centre of the village, then picked up my phone and handbag lying on the passenger seat. As I did so, the phone went ping in my hand. I tapped in my security code to check the screen.

'COLEEN PATRICIA FENSOME,' it said, in familiar capital letters. 'U BETTER WATCH URSELF COS I'M GOING 2 STALK U AND FIND U THEN RAPE U.'

I dropped the phone as if it was a red-hot coal. My mouth went dry and my heart thumped. The Twitter name was different but it was the same capital letters and the same use of my married name. It had to be the same person. I felt so exposed and vulnerable. Was he in the car park? Was he watching me? I locked the car door from the inside and looked frantically about. Suddenly the centre of my beautiful, friendly village looked as dangerous as the mean streets of New York.

I picked up the phone and called Ray. 'Get home now,' he insisted. 'This is ridiculous, Col. You've got to go to the police.'

In the end, I left it to Antony and Duncan, although

my details were added to the police file. What else could I do? As soon as you report or block somebody they can simply start a new account under a different name. Who knew where the culprit was from? He wasn't even necessarily in the UK. I read later that some women politicians and a famous historian called Mary Beard had been sent similar messages – all warning of a bomb that would go off at 22.47. It was chilling but I was determined that one idiot wasn't going to rob me of my Twitter friends.

Twitter can be an amazingly good place. I don't know what I would have done without it during those days immediately after Bernie's death. But it can also be a very scary place, where nutters can hide behind online profiles to bully, harass or abuse you. It's one of the things that Ray and I can still get into a fight about.

'For fuck's sake, Col,' he'll say. 'You wouldn't dream of making your mobile number public so that people could text you whatever twisted message they fancied. Having a Twitter account isn't any different. It's like an open invitation to every Tom, Dick or Harry that wants to take a shot at you.'

He's right, of course. Being on Twitter does leave you vulnerable to some very odd types. But I've decided that I'm not going to let them chase me off the site. Stress-induced eczema or not, I have too much fun on Twitter with my genuine followers to give it up.

I like the way people who are interested in me can ask questions and talk to me directly. One of the things

I was asked on Twitter a lot at the time was whether I would ever return to *Loose Women*. It was a very good question. It had taken a little while for the novelty of not having to travel to London to do the show to wear off. But, after a few months, I had started to miss it. There is something really comforting about *Loose Women* – the audience, the camaraderie you feel with the other girls – and I guess I always knew that I might be pulled back to it one day.

For some time now I'd been doing a weekly agony-aunt spot on *The Alan Titchmarsh Show* back at the old *Loose Women* South Bank studios. Each week I was there I'd bump into former colleagues, floor managers or makeup girls, who would ask if I'd ever consider returning to *Loose Women*. I couldn't say it at the time but that was exactly what was just around the corner.

Just a few days earlier a phone call had come in from ITV asking me whether I'd be interested in returning. The show was going through a line-up change and was in the papers every day, with speculation about who was joining and who was leaving. I found out that ITV had asked me and Kaye Adams back at the same time. I've always thought Kaye is a brilliant presenter who can as easily interview the prime minister as she can an *X-Factor* contestant, and we've always been great friends. The idea of returning with her was irresistible. It also felt like just what I needed after everything that had gone on. It felt like I'd be coming home.

And other reasons made the offer attractive. The new mix of panelists, Lisa Maxwell, Linda Robson, Janet

Street-Porter, Sherrie Hewson and Jane McDonald, sounded exciting. The changes made the programme feel fresh and I knew we'd all get on.

But the biggest reason by far behind my decision to return was Bernie. I could hear her voice telling me to move on and get back to work. She had such an amazing work ethic – Bernie was performing flat out even when she knew she was dying. She battled on and on and refused to give up. I could hear her saying, 'Life bloody goes on. Get back out there and do what you do.'

So, when Neil started talking to me about going back, I immediately said yes. To be honest, *Loose Women* is the one show where I can totally be myself. I think I'm better at that than anything else. I'd much rather chatter on naturally than stick to a script or play a part. I loved the studio audience and the viewers at home. They'd stood by me after my divorce from Shane, never cared whether I was fat or thin or somewhere in between. Everyone else seemed to have an opinion on my shape and size but not the *Loose Women* fans. They had always been so warm and welcoming, I couldn't wait to get back to them.

I was getting ready to do *Titchmarsh* the day before the official announcement when the subject came up. 'Have you thought of going back on *Loose Women*?' asked Donna, the lovely makeup girl.

'Er, yeah, I suppose I have,' I said cautiously, trying hard not to let the secret slip out. I'm such a bad liar I felt sure she would guess the truth. 'If they asked me.'

'You should just tell them that,' said Donna. 'It would be great to see you back there.'

Twenty-four hours later, when ITV finally made the big announcement, Donna was one of the first to text me: *You lying bitch!* she wrote. *Can't believe you didn't tell me – but glad to hear you're coming back!*

I sent her a grovelling text: *I'm so sorry! Was sworn to secrecy! Forgive me?*

*Of course! Good luck!* she replied.

The next two weeks were frantic. I had clothes to buy, childcare arrangements to make, train tickets to sort out. This time around it was going to be so much easier. I'd been offered two alternate days on the panel, which meant I could get the early train to London, do the show and be back home in Wilmslow by four thirty the same day. Most people have jobs that take them out of the house from eight to six, so it seemed like a doddle. Ciara was thrilled to hear I was going back to the show – she'd always loved it and could see I was happy about it. Excitedly, we made plans – on the days I was working, I'd meet her after school and we'd go off to the stables together to see Paddy and Orla. The rest of the week I'd be home all the time. It was perfect.

'If that's what you want, Col, go for it,' Ray said, when I told him. 'You've always been brilliant on that show. But perhaps you can be a bit more discreet about our sex life this time?' Probably not, I thought.

*

October 7, my first day, rolled around and I was very nervous. It had been two and a half years since I'd left the show. So much had happened in that time that I was worried I might not be able to cope. Plus, I hadn't made it easy on myself. That first day was going to start at seven fifteen in Hair and Makeup at the *Daybreak* studio for an interview with Lorraine Kelly. Then it was on to *Loose Women* for my very first show.

What a day that was! Lorraine was as lovely as ever. She had always been close to Bernie and I could see she was genuinely still so very sad about my sister's death. 'It's great to have you back with us,' she said warmly. 'Bernie was so very, very special and I know she would have wanted to see you back on screen.' I understood what she meant. But that nice thought didn't stop my hands trembling. I was shaking in my boots.

'Och,' she said, in her lovely Scottish accent. 'I can't believe you're nervous. I'm going to be watching you with a cup of tea and a packet of biscuits and after two minutes it will be as if you've never been away.'

I prayed she was right. As soon as I'd finished filming *Daybreak* I was whisked off to the *Loose Women* studios. And, oh, my God, it was like coming home. Everybody gave me such a lovely welcome. From the production team to the presenters and the people in the canteen, they were all great. I felt like I'd been away from my mates and was slipping seamlessly back in.

Kaye wasn't due to start for another couple of

weeks so my first show back was anchored by the lovely Andrea McLean. Alongside me on the desk were Linda Robson – who is great on the show and to me will always be Tracey from the brilliant *Birds of a Feather* – and my old friend Sherrie Hewson. Not much had changed. As I took the same old seat on the left-hand side of the panel, I was immediately comfortable. It just felt right.

And it got better and better. Those old Sunday-night pit-of-the-stomach blues I used to feel completely disappeared. Pretty soon I was rushing off for the early train looking forward to being on *Loose Women*. It was such a relief because, by the end of my previous run, I had been dreading it.

By the time Kaye rejoined the gang the show was like it had been in the good old days. The atmosphere was fantastic and we all really genuinely got on. Kaye and I have the same sarcastic sense of humour and, off screen, we'd call each other all the names under the sun. By the second week she'd started having a go at me during the show. Well, Twitter went into overdrive.

'Kaye Adams, leave Coleen alone. Stop bullying her!' Dozens of messages flooded in. I had to put out a tweet to rescue her.

'We're best mates, it's only a laugh, honest!' I told my feisty followers. It's funny what they do and don't see in the on-screen relationships between all the girls.

One of the nice surprises was how well I got on with Janet Street-Porter. To be frank, I was scared to death of her the first time we were on the show together. But she turned out to be really lovely. She likes to give off this gruff exterior, but underneath she's as kind and gentle as anything.

We are absolute chalk and cheese but we seem to get on like a house on fire. I asked her once why she liked me. 'You make me laugh,' she said. Of course, it's not just our personalities that are so different. I'm short and round and soft. She's tall, angular and dresses beautifully. We look really funny alongside each other.

Since being back on screen regularly I've become more accepting about the weight thing. It's just another priority that I've reassessed since Bernie's death. I'm tired of constantly giving myself a hard time about it. Yes, it felt good to be a size twelve and I loved the way regular exercise and training made my body feel toned and lean, but, honestly, these days I'm just as happy with a cup of tea and a packet of chocolate digestives. I like to think I'm still fit, though. Mucking out Orla and riding with Ciara is as tough a workout as anything I've ever done. Sometimes we get back from the stables and it's all I can do to crawl into a hot bath to ease my aching muscles.

The pressure's still on for women on television to be a certain shape. If I get a bad tweet or a nasty comment in the press, it's always about my weight. I'm fed up feeling like I should disappear from the TV screens just because I'm not a size eight. Not long after my return to *Loose Women* I decided I was going to be proud of my body. If that means being a poster girl for normal-sized women, then so be it!

For three years I managed to keep off the five stone that I lost in 2007. In 2008 I received the best compliment of my life when I was namechecked for a second time by a *Coronation Street* character. This time, a lad called Graeme Proctor suddenly declared in the Rovers, 'That Coleen Nolan's fit.'

I was watching the soap at home and my ears pricked up.

'You're joking, she's old enough to be your mum,' said his mate, David Platt.

'Exactly. Knows what she's doing,' replied Graeme. Oh, my God! I nearly passed out with excitement.

But having soap characters gossiping about my weight just increased the pressure to maintain a size twelve. I felt as if there were so many eyes on me, just waiting for me to get bigger again. Gradually, I started to relax about how much I was eating and some of the weight slowly came back. I was depressed about it at first, but Ray soon snapped me out of it.

'So what if you've put on a bit of weight?' he said to me one night, after I'd been moaning about not being able to fit into anything in my wardrobe. 'You still look beautiful and you'll always be beautiful to me.'

Just hearing him say those words, it was as if a cloud had lifted. Since sorting out our marriage hiccup in 2010, our love life is very much back on track. Knowing Ray finds me attractive makes me feel sexy. I have boobs and a bum and I still go in and out in the right places, I like to think. I've stopped trying to squeeze into inappropriate skinny dresses and leather trousers. I think the important thing is to know what flatters your shape and stick to the rules. For me that means minimizing my bust with a V-neck top and always going for three-quarter-length sleeves, rather than spaghetti straps. I nip my waist in with a belt to get as close to an hour-glass shape as I can.

After all, the average-sized woman in the UK is a fourteen to sixteen. Which is me! That's why I was so pleased when Marisota first asked me to design my range. I wanted to find clothes that were fun and sexy without being tight and tarty. They also had to flatter women who were perhaps bigger than a model size. And I was determined to find an answer to the old problem of bigger boobs. When you've got breasts as large as mine, shopping can be a nightmare. Clothes that hoist them up or are tight-fitting just make you look enormous. I don't necessarily want to show them off – sometimes it's better to put them away!

The Marisota job made me realize the importance of confidence and self-esteem. Ray once told me, 'You know, I'd put personality over looks every time. You can get bored with somebody's appearance after a while – but you can fall in love with somebody you find funny and interesting.' It was a bit of a back-handed compliment but I know what he meant.

Growing older also makes you feel more confident. Ageing may bring with it a few aches and pains and the odd complaining joint, but it also makes you realize that you don't care as much as you used to about what people are thinking. I like the fact that I'm not as aware of myself as I used to be. Years ago, when I was a skinny little thing in the Nolans, I'd worry about wearing the right clothes or having the correct hairstyle for the time. Now I don't give a stuff! I'll always have my insecurities – there will always be some girl who walks past, like Danica, my gorgeous *Celebrity Big Brother* housemate, and makes you feel fat and frumpy – but these days I try to remember what's important. And having a model figure isn't really.

It's especially difficult once your sons start bringing home drop-dead gorgeous girls. Whenever I see Emma, Shane's beautiful girlfriend, I always think, Can you just go back to bed and wake up a little bit uglier, a bit fatter, and with your legs four inches shorter? But, really, I love looking at my kids and their friends. They are so gorgeous, so full of life and excited about the future. And that's how it should be. I think about the dreadful time we went through as a family last year and I'm glad they still feel such optimism.

Bernie's death has changed the way I think about so many things. Mostly, it has shown me the importance of love and family. There have been too many rifts in the Nolan family, too many wasted years filled with bickering and cold silences. Our parents taught us that blood is thicker than water and that, whatever happened, the Nolans should stick together. I don't believe that any more but what I do know is that Bernie would have wanted us brothers and sisters to be happy together. It's about time we did something about that . . .

# Chapter Twelve

Once upon a time there were Tommy, Anne, Denise, Maureen, Brian, Linda, Bernie and me. My God, eight kids. What a handful we could have been. But our parents were so strict we simply didn't dare to run wild. Mum and Dad could keep us in line with just a look. Yes, there would be the occasional smack from him or a clip round the ear from her but, really, we were all so frightened of our parents that we never got into any serious bother.

Dad was especially strict with the three eldest girls. Poor Anne, Denise and Maureen bore the brunt of his overprotectiveness, and offstage, even as adults, were still wearing knee-length socks and not a scrap of makeup. Anne didn't leave home until she married her husband, Brian – by then she was almost thirty! Maureen and Denise, too, were in their twenties before they cut the apron strings and bolted for independence. At the Oxford, the Blackpool pub they would occasionally escape to, they were known as the Three Wise Virgins.

But it was a very different story for me. In many ways I have always felt a little removed from the rest of the family. For a start, I was the only one born in England – all the others started life in Dublin. Then there's the fact that by the time I was in my teens the girls were performing all over the world and I was left behind in Blackpool to live with my brothers and my auntie Theresa. I was really independent from an early age – I even had my own house by the time I was seventeen. While the other girls were being managed and looked after by my dad, I was the lone bird who had somehow managed to fly the coop.

I mention this now because I think that's what may lie behind some of the rows that we've famously had. I know I had it easy. By the time he got to me, Dad couldn't be bothered to lay down the law – he'd done it with seven others, he'd had enough. I got away with plenty of things the others would have been in big trouble over, including being the first daughter to have a baby out of wedlock. I can still remember nervously telling my auntie Theresa and her saying, 'Oh, Jesus, I don't envy you telling your mum and dad.'

But to everyone's astonishment, Dad was fine. 'As long as you're happy, I'm happy,' he said, when Shane and I spilled the beans that Shane Junior was on his way.

Mum was more upset, but simply said, 'So, you'll be getting married, then?'

As I grew up and moved away from the rest of them, I no longer swallowed that old Nolan motto that the family was all that mattered. The brainwashing our parents had done to all of us had long since ceased to have an effect, and I hated the way the Nolans would try to cover up their problems rather than face them. When Anne and Ray had the original argument back in 2007, I wasn't willing to put my sisters before my husband.

'If Ray's wrong I'll tell him and we'll have to deal with it,' I remember saying to Anne. 'But this time I know that he's not. He's completely innocent so my loyalty's with him.' I was the first one to stand my ground and Anne and Denise despised that.

Denise was the most pissed off and I put that down to her own childhood. She and Mum had a really strange relationship. They loved one another but they really clashed, mainly because they were carved out of one another, like two peas in a pod. She also had a lot of issues with Dad. She idolized him but they rowed constantly up until the day he died. They never got to iron out their problems and I am sure that's difficult to cope with. What's more, poor Denise grew up feeling anxious about her looks. Linda was always described as the naughty Nolan, while Maureen was the pretty one. With Denise, unkind people would occasionally say, 'Oh, you're the ugly one with the great voice,' and, understandably, it crushed her. People can be extremely cruel.

So, for one reason or another, I've always felt that Denise resented me. Maybe she envied my upbringing, my independence and my relationship with our parents. It might have been hard to watch my early success and the big house that Shane and I had together, and then I think she might have envied my second burst of fame later on. Once we were playing bingo together and I won a fiver. Bloody hell, she even resented that! As soon as my hand shot up and I shouted, 'House!' she slammed her pen down on the table. 'God, I might have known it would be you.' I'll never forget the venom in her voice. When she jumped into the row between Anne and Ray it made life very unpleasant for everyone. She was bringing up things from years earlier so this resentment seemed to be long and bitterly held.

Denise and I got on great as kids but I remember having to be careful about what I said or did. If I chose to spend time with someone other than her she would really take it to heart and there would be hell to pay.

'I can't believe you'd rather be with your friends than with your own sister,' she'd sulk. There was no consoling her but by the time I became an adult I'd had enough. I was no longer prepared to drop everything for her.

While the war of words was raging over Anne's supposed tour snub, she published some terrible things about me on her website. I was so upset to see them. 'Ray has done what no one inside the family, or out of it, has ever tried to do,' Denise wrote. And also, 'My parents, although they had faults, made us believe in the maxim that family has to come first. They would not be proud of the 2009 Nolans' tour. They would be ashamed. The tour is immoral.'

Worse still, she tore a strip off Linda, Maureen and Bernie for putting us before her and Anne. 'They have gone along with a man they have known for nine years, and his wife – MY SISTER,' she posted on her site.

When Bernie was ill we both did our best to come to an uneasy truce. But once Bernie had died the truce appeared to be over. I read on her website just recently that she doubts we can ever be friends. It's sad.

There has been a lot written about the Nolans' so-called reunion and how Bernie's death has brought us together again. I hate to be the one to spoil that particular fairy tale but it's not entirely true. I believe that Denise continues to resent me and I'm not sure how we can ever get over that. I could never invite her to my house in Cheshire because I know she wouldn't be happy for me. I'm fed up feeling guilty for what I've achieved.

People say that life's too short to spend it squabbling with those you love. It is: Bernie taught us this, absolutely. But it's also too short to spend your life being made to feel sad or guilty by somebody who supposedly loves you. I'm not going to do it any more.

It was partly because of my relationship with Denise that we left Blackpool in the first place. Our house stood on the corner of a road and for months we'd been plagued by noisy teenagers who were using our wall as a meeting place and a public loo. One night they even vandalized our cars. It was enough to make us want to leave but the ill feeling between Denise and I made the situation even worse.

'I can't stand it here any longer,' I told Ray. 'I can't go anywhere without bumping into Denise. I'd rather put some distance between us.' As soon as we moved into the house in Wilmslow, it was as if a weight had been lifted from my shoulders.

Bernie was reconciled with Anne and Denise before she died. I'm glad about that. And the other girls are now the best of mates as well – they are back together again and going to the bingo! Linda and Denise only live about four doors apart in Blackpool so it can't have been easy. I'm glad for them. But I think it's only been possible because the other girls are willing to fit in with Denise. It seems to me that even if they don't want to do something they will fall in with her plans. They can't bear the trauma it will cause if they cross her. And I'm not doing that any longer.

On a happier note, Anne and I have kissed and made up. We'd already had a hug at the funeral and were at Bernie's hotel send-off when our eyes met across the room. Anne came over, carrying a drink for me.

'Hi, Col.' She smiled. 'So, what are we going to do now?'

I looked at her and remembered all the years when she had virtually raised me. She was like a second mum to me and I loved her dearly. We were so close that we shared a single bed until I was fourteen and she was twenty-nine!

'I don't have a problem, Anne,' I said. 'I know you want to be loyal to Denise but none of that matters to me. My door will always be open to you.'

Her eyes were smiling and she touched my arm. 'Let's get on with it, then,' she said. 'I missed too many years of Bernie's life, I don't want to be without you, too.'

A week later she came to the house for the first time

ever. It was lovely to see her sitting in my kitchen drinking tea and it felt entirely natural. We had slipped back into being sisters again without an ounce of difficulty. Maureen, Linda and my nieces also came over and we had a girly night in. It was great.

At the height of the row, Anne had spoken to the *Daily Mail* and disowned us all. 'I have no sisters now,' she'd said. That had been a particularly dark day. So I was pleased when she did another interview with the paper, describing how we had put our bickering behind us. It was sad, though, to read how isolated she had felt.

'The others talked about times they'd spent together at Bernie's house while I was still sulking at home, and I felt sick with remorse that I'd created a situation that meant I couldn't share those memories,' she said. 'How I wished then I could turn the clock back.'

Maureen, the peacemaker as always, is very pleased to have most of her family on speaking terms again. When we were kids, she was always the laid-back one. She was kind and soft and would see the goodness in somebody even if they were obviously a wrong 'un. She's like that today – too soft for her own good.

Maureen never stops working and I've been thrilled about her success in the musical *Blood Brothers*. That show's become a bit of a Nolan phenomenon. Maureen, Denise, Bernie and Linda are in *The Guinness Book of Records* for being the most siblings to have played the same role – that of Willy Russell's tragic Liverpool mum Mrs Johnstone. First Bernie played her back in

1998, then Denise up until 2004, next up was Linda from 2006 until 2008 and Maureen seems to have been playing her off and on for almost ten years! I've often wondered if I could follow in their footsteps but I'd be too terrified of letting them down. I don't want to be the Nolan to mess it all up!

Then there's Linda ... Amazingly, at the age of fifty-three, she is about to become a mum! She's going through the process of – hopefully – being approved as a foster parent. If all goes to plan there are going to be some very lucky kids out there.

When we were growing up, Linda was the one who was mad for babies. She even did a childcare O level at school. Bernie, Maureen and I would always tease her about being like a clucking mother hen.

'You're going to end up with eight, just like Mum,' Bernie would say. But, sadly, it wasn't to be. Although Linda and her husband Brian were blissfully happy it never seemed like the right time for her to take a break from performing and start a family. I know she bitterly regrets that now. She's a fantastic auntie to Erin and Ciara and their cousins, but she wishes she hadn't left it too late to have babies of her own.

So, we can't wait to see her surrounded by children, giving them the love and support they need. It will be amazing for her and no more than she deserves. Life has been tough for Linda. She's the one who has suffered and had more loss in her life than any of us. First she discovered she had advanced breast cancer and went through all that gruelling chemo treatment, then her lovely Brian died. And, although it sounds a bit odd to say it, I think she has been hit the hardest by Bernie's death.

There were only thirteen months between Linda and Bernie and they were inseparable. They were more like twins and would spend hours together, practising their singing and swapping clothes or makeup. When Bernie was diagnosed for the second time and we knew the future looked grim, Linda was devastated and felt desperately guilty.

'It's not fair, Col,' she said to me one day, when we were sitting in the day room at the Trinity Hospice when Bernie was very sick. 'It should be me lying in that bed.'

'Don't be ridiculous, what on earth are you talking about?' I asked her.

'I miss Brian every day of my life,' she said honestly. 'I don't have him, I don't have children. There really isn't much for me to live for.' I was appalled and I knew that Bernie would be, too.

'Well, you'd better shut up because Bernie would kill you if she heard you,' I told her. It was so upsetting to know she felt that way. Poor Linda.

For a while, the 2009 tour was a great distraction for her and it was then that I saw the first signs of the old Linda emerging. But Bernie's death dragged her back to a very dark place indeed. I'm so glad for her that she has something joyful to look forward to. I can't wait to see her devoting her life to little ones – just as we once imagined she would be.

Linda's also been talking about us touring again. She would love us to do the concerts that Bernie had dreamed of the year before her death. She's even worked out how we could take Bernie on the road with us.

'I can see it now,' she told me excitedly. 'We'll have Bernie projected on to the stage so that she can perform with us. It'll be amazing.'

That was a really exciting idea, but on the other hand Bernie was so looking forward to doing one last Nolans' tour that it would seem wrong to do it without her. It would upset me too much to think of her missing out. Perhaps in the future it might feel the right thing to do but without Bernie, it just wouldn't be the same. There is also the danger that another tour would stir up all the old rows over whether Anne should be involved. Now I've made up with her I'd hate to fall out for the sake of a four-week tour. But, as difficult as it would be for her, the line-up wouldn't change because that was Bernie's tour and a new tour would be with her, somehow, one way or another. Bernie can't be replaced, so the line-up would stay the same and I hope Anne would understand that.

As I come to the close of this book I realize that, quite by chance, I have come full circle. Somehow – and I can't actually believe I'm writing this – I had let myself be persuaded to take part in the 2014 series of *Dancing On Ice*. Yes, the show that had caused me sleepless nights, bruises and a near-calamitous back injury, was knocking on my door again. Why couldn't I just say no?

The nightmare returned in September, just before I was invited back on to *Loose Women*. As these things usually do, it all started with a call from Neil.

'Hi, Coleen. Now, I know you won't want to hear this . . .' he began. Uh-oh, I thought, what's he got me into now? '. . . but there's going to be one last series of *Dancing On Ice* and the producers want it to be all the previous winners and viewers' favourites. They've included you in that. What do you think?'

What did I think? I thought I'd rather stick pins in my eyes. But part of me was really flattered, too. I loved everything about the show. I just hated doing the damn skating.

'Erm, it's lovely to be considered,' I said. 'But I haven't been on the ice since the last show four years ago. I think my skating days may be over.'

Neil asked me to think about it. I think I knew deep down that it wasn't the right time for me to do a full-on show like *Dancing On Ice*, but on the other hand it was lovely of them to ask and it had really changed my life the first time I appeared, so I was torn . . .

I texted him back. *Can't believe I'm saying this*, I wrote, *but let's at least have a conversation with them.* I could just imagine him smiling at the other end of the phone. You idiot, Nolan! I thought. You've really done it now.

At first the more I heard, the more the terrors began to fade. Neil suggested that this time round I would just have fun. I would be competing against some of the best-ever contestants – fantastic skaters like Ray Quinn, and *Emmerdale*'s Suzanne Shaw and Hayley

Tamaddon. I wouldn't stand a chance against any of them so, right from the off, there would be no pressure. It brought back memories of the first time round, when I was worried that the viewers might continue to vote for me and that we'd end up in the ridiculous position of me beating Ray Quinn in the final.

Back then, my own Ray was starting to get worried, too. 'I'm not being funny, Col, but I don't want you to win it. That would be a joke,' he said. 'Compared to Ray Quinn, you're just not good. It would be embarrassing!' And he was right. This time around I'd be outnumbered by quality skaters, I could be there just to make up the numbers.

'As long as Todd Carty doesn't show me up.' I laughed, remembering the lumbering performances of the ex-*EastEnders* star. Even I could do better than that, I hoped, and I was willing to take part if it gave the viewers a laugh.

But it wasn't long before the same old fears started to emerge. I still had rib injuries from skating in 2009. My back has never been the same since, plus the stables accident had left me with a rod in my finger. I dreaded falling on to the hard ice, breaking a finger and seeing the metal pins poking out! I could go through the agony of six months' training only to break my leg or get kicked off in the first week, I thought.

No sooner had I said yes than the sleepless nights started all over again. *Dancing On Ice* was in my thoughts all day every day. Each time I received a text from the physio or the trainer my stomach would lurch and I would feel physically sick. I've got to get myself out of this, I thought. I've got to tell Neil and he'll have to tell them. Poor Neil – always the messenger!

Bernie's death has made me see that life is too short to feel scared all the time. I'd been so stressed – over Bernie, the rows with Denise, the Twitter threats and now *Dancing On Ice*. Why am I doing this to myself? I wondered. Why put myself through even more anxiety? By October I could stand it no longer. I was staying overnight in a London hotel and getting ready to slob on the bed with a plate of room-service pasta when I received a text from the show's organizers telling me I had a final boot fitting on 15 October. I'd been putting off making a decision. Now I realized I'd have to be brave and just tell Neil that I wanted out.

But, weirdly enough, the next morning he phoned me. 'It's about *Dancing On Ice*,' he said.

'You just saying those words makes me feel a bit nauseous,' I wailed.

'Well, today is Last Chance Saloon as far as signing the contract is concerned,' he warned. 'We can't hold off any longer.' My stomach lurched, did a little somersault and landed again, making me feel sick. Then, incredibly, I heard him say, 'But, to be honest, I've been thinking it over and I really don't think you are ready to do this, and you need more time at home. If your heart isn't in it one hundred per cent it's just not worth putting yourself through it. You had such an amazing experience on the show the first time, let's leave it as the wonderful memory it is. Now you can just continue to take the time out you need to get yourself together after everything that's gone on.'

Hallelujah! It was like winning the lottery! I almost wept with relief. This is why Neil is such an amazing manager as well as friend. No one has ever looked after me as well as he does, and besides Ray, he's the other man who always looks out for my best interests. I always feel safe knowing he's got my back.

When I look back now, I don't know what I was thinking. By the time the show went live I'd have been forty-nine. My fitness is a million per cent poorer than it was in 2009. I would have had to have a personal trainer to build up the strength in my poor old knackered back. I know how it happened: in this business you say yes to things because you're never sure where the next job is coming from. I was kidding myself that I wanted to embrace the challenge and not refuse anything, especially a show I love so much. But I should have listened to the little voice inside my head that, at the very mention of *Dancing On Ice*, was screaming, *Nooooooooo!*

# Epilogue

Remember the old fortune-teller on Venice Beach? I'll never forget her. Her terrible warning will be etched upon my heart for ever, and not a day goes by that I don't dream of retracing my steps all the way back to California and hearing a very different future.

But her predictions about Bernie were not the only thing she passed on to me that day. She also mentioned Ray and my career, and in both respects she's been proven right.

'I don't know what you do for a living but you're working on something soon for a lot of money. It won't lead to what you hoped for and it will be a hard year but after that justice will prevail,' she'd said.

Looking back, it's almost laughable how accurate she was. A few months later I would be sitting in a house full of strangers, being driven mad by a diva called Julie Goodyear but knowing that the *Big Brother* experience was buying me some time to be with my family. That was what she'd meant by 'a lot of money'. The *Celebrity Big Brother* pay cheque allowed me to take a year off and have those months at home with Ray, Ciara and the boys. It was, as she said, a hard year, but I'm so glad I was able to be by Bernie's side at the Blackpool hospice. I hate to think what it would have been like trying to juggle that with the demands of TV in London.

As for justice prevailing, well, I'm back on *Loose Women* doing what I love most. It's not an obvious kind of justice, but I feel as if I'm doing justice to myself. For too long I convinced myself that I was happy to be away from television. That seems like a mistake now, especially as I can combine this amazing show with being at home so much with Ray and Ciara. It feels like a fresh start, doing a job I enjoy with colleagues I respect and get along with. I couldn't be happier.

The fortune-teller also told me that Ray would come up trumps. 'Your husband is going to be amazing. He'll support you every step of the way,' she said. And when I really and truly needed him, on the day of Bernie's funeral, he was there for me. When I didn't think I was going to be able to walk out of the Grand Theatre into the sunshine, he literally did just that – he supported me every step of the way.

Whether that's coincidence or some sort of gypsy power I don't know. But I will never go to a fortune-teller again. I'd rather live my life in blissful ignorance.

I started writing this book a year ago, but when we heard Bernie's terrible diagnosis I thought I would put it to one side and never return to it. But in truth it has really helped me through these dark and difficult months, being able to turn to these pages to pour out my feelings. I'm sure it's going to read very personally for you because it is a very personal book for me, and now I'm so glad I did it because it has helped keep me sane. As I now know, there are many, many people who have experienced similar losses to my own. The woman who approached me in the supermarket, the Twitter followers who tweeted that they had been inconsolable since the death of their brother or sister or mother. I really do think that by sharing these major life hurdles we can learn to clear them a little more easily. I truly hope my story helps anyone struggling with bereavement or the torment of breast-cancer treatment.

Since *Upfront & Personal* was published, I've had one wobble after another. There's been the self-doubt over my weight, the near catastrophic blow to my marriage and, of course, the absolute tragedy that was the death of my sister. While I'd give anything to have her with us still, I'm so grateful to Bernie. Her lust for life and her determination to keep going is a real lesson to me and one that I'm going to hold close for ever.

There have been other lessons, too. Through *Big Brother* I've learned that I care about what people think of me – perhaps a bit too much. And while I can't do anything about that it has made me less judgemental of others. I know how much it hurts when you're being publicly criticized and I won't be doing as much of that as I used to. It will be a different Coleen Nolan sitting on the *Loose Women* panel – one who thinks more carefully before she opens her mouth. And through my work as an agony aunt I've learned to see other people's point of view. When someone pisses me off I don't instantly take offence. I stop and ask myself what answer I would give on my page in the *Mirror*.

I've learned to appreciate what I have. So often I find myself thinking, Bernie would have loved to be doing this now. It makes me sadder than I can tell you. Then I give myself a kick up the bum and tell myself to get on with it. That's what Bernie would have done.

This being the first year since her death, there have been many milestones to pass. The first birthday without her, the first Christmas, the anniversary of her death. Every family celebration is painful without her, and each time I look at Erin, who is growing into a beautiful young woman, I mourn for what Bernie will not have.

Erin's getting on brilliantly, thank God. Children are amazingly resilient and, while I don't doubt that she thinks about her mum every single day, I know that Erin is slowly bouncing back and will seize hold of her future in the same way that Bernie did. The apple didn't fall far from the tree with that one.

Steve is finding it difficult. He leans on Linda more and more. She and our brother Brian – who lost his wife Linzie just two years into their marriage – are perhaps the only ones who really know how he feels. Linda says that Steve puts on a brave face but that he has sobbed his heart out to her on more than one occasion.

'Does it ever get any better?' he's asked her. I think, for Linda, it's beginning to, but it has taken her more than seven years. Grief is so hard to endure.

Wherever I go, people still say how sorry they are about Bernie and ask me questions about her. This, then, is a chance for me to put it all in a book and tell them. I want to shout about her from the rooftop. I never want people to forget her.

Losing Bernie has affected us all in very different ways. We've all learned so much and we miss her every moment of every day. For me, her death was a ground-shaking, heart-stopping confirmation that life is for living and families are for loving. And for that, my beautiful Bernie, I will always be grateful.

Coleen x

# Acknowledgements

To Penguin, especially Fenella Bates, for all your support and patience. Thank you so much. To my manager Neil Howarth. What can I say? Your loyalty, encouragement and belief in me is never-ending and I'm thankful for all you are and for all you do, my friend for ever. To Nick and Paul (my bezzies) for being true friends through thick and thin, and especially for all the laughter. To my wonderful husband Ray, we've been through so much together – good and bad – but each challenge just makes us stronger. I love you with all my heart. And lastly, to all my family for making me the person I am today, especially my beautiful sister Bernie, who I miss every moment of every day. I've learnt so much from your courage and strength, and whenever I'm unsure about anything I always ask myself, 'What would Bernie do?' and I know that you'll be looking down and saying, 'Just bloody get on with it and live life to the full!'

# Picture Permissions

Bernie and I © Nicky Johnston and Universal; My *Dancing On Ice* partner Stuart Widdall © REX/Ken McKay/ITV; Action shots from *Dancing On Ice* © REX/Ken McKay/ITV; The Nolans tour photoshoot images © Nicky Johnston and Universal; The Nolans, 1974 © Alpha General/Press Association Images; Keith Lemon on *This Morning* © REX; Barry Manilow on *This Morning* © REX/Ken McKay; *Celebrity Big Brother* launch night © PA/Press Association Images; Leaving the *Celebrity Big Brother* House © PA/Press Association Images; Julie Goodyear, Ashley McKenzie and I © REX; all other photographs © Coleen Nolan.